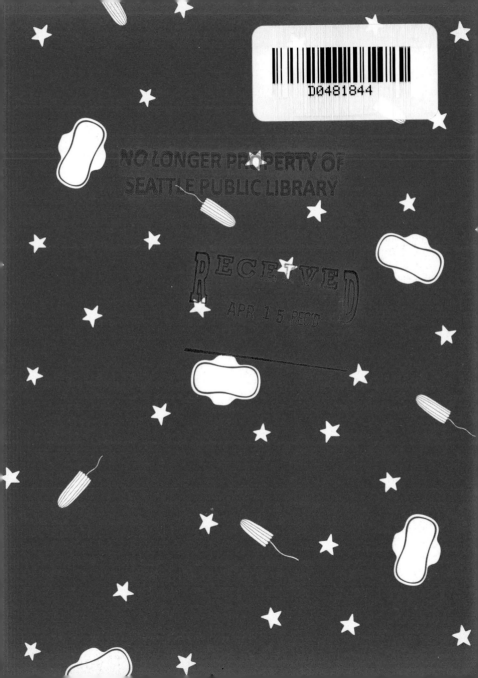

D0481844

The publisher thanks Sukriti Dabral of Partners
in Sex Education for reviewing the US edition.

First US edition 2021
First published by Hardie Grant Egmont (Australia) 2019

Library of Congress Catalog Card Number pending
ISBN 978-1-5362-1476-5 (hardcover)
ISBN 978-1-5362-1477-2 (paperback)

20 21 22 23 24 25 LEO 10 9 8 7 6 5 4 3 2 1

Printed in Heshan, Guangdong, China

This book was typeset in Nexa Slab.
The illustrations were created digitally.

Walker Books US
a division of
Candlewick Press
99 Dover Street
Somerville, Massachusetts 02144

www.walkerbooksus.com

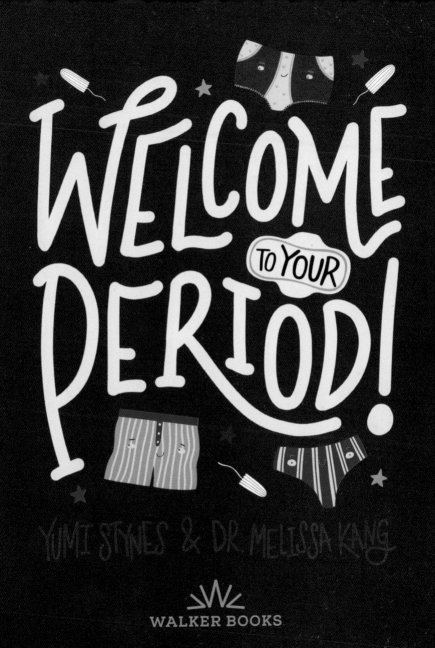

WELCOME TO YOUR PERIOD!

YUMI STYNES & DR. MELISSA KANG

WALKER BOOKS

To the next generation of bleeders, may you kick ass and have many laughs. And to their mothers, who try to protect their children from all pain but fail, and fail gloriously.

Yumi

To Julian, Samantha, Georgia, and Hannah-Rose, who learned a lot of stuff but taught me more

Melissa

start here

How do you use this book?

Short answer — any way you like!

Let's start by saying that it is *totally OK* to be excited or scared or nervous about getting your period. *Of course.* It's all new, right? But no matter what your situation, this book will give you the info you need to handle your period like a boss.

There's a lot in here, and you don't need to get your head around all of it right away. You can read this book cover to cover or dip in to find the most interesting parts.

You probably just want to get to the stuff that you need to know right now.

If you're starting from scratch and want to know what a period even *is*, go to "The Basics" on page 4.

If you want to know the difference between pads and tampons (and how to use them), go to page 42.

And if you're interested in what's happening behind the scenes in your body, check out pages 122 and 148.

There's also a vocab section on page 154 in case you need a refresher!

Over the next few years, the things you want to know may change. That's OK — this book will still be here when you need it. Parts you didn't think you needed to read will suddenly become relevant.

And when you feel like you're a period boss, you can share this book with your sister, cousin, or friend and say,

"Welcome to your period! Guess what? It's going to be totally fine."

Contents

Welcome
TO YOUR
Period

Hi!

So glad you're here.
WELCOME to your period!

Listen, I want to tell you something (this is Yumi speaking). When I was a kid, it was tricky finding honest info about periods. But the one place I could go was a health column in *Dolly* (an Australian magazine for teenagers) called "Dolly Doctor."

"Dolly Doctor" was a regular Q&A with a real doctor who specialized in girl problems. You could write in to ask her advice, and she never laughed at the questions or made fun of you or even flinched — no matter *what* you asked. Best of all, her answers were spot-on 100 percent of the time!

If you had told me that one day I would be cowriting a book about periods with one of those columnists, I would have screamed with disbelief and happiness!

Even though she is totally up on the science now, periods were a complete mystery to Dr. Melissa when she first got hers. And they were to me too.

To learn about periods, Dr. Melissa had to watch an excruciating video at school in fifth grade. Everyone in the class was so embarrassed; they couldn't say anything or even look at one another. After that, her mom had ONE talk with her about periods and that was it.

My own mom wordlessly handed me a free pamphlet written by a pad manufacturer, and that was pretty much our "talk" about periods — but to tell you the truth, I wasn't too fazed. I secretly thought I probably wouldn't get my period at all, ever — because I *really* didn't want to, so why the heck should I?!

Dr. Melissa and I found out that a lot of girls feel the same way. And as we matured, we both wanted to be more open about periods, learn as much as we could, and talk about them without shame. Getting your period is not only natural and really common, but also pretty interesting and even exciting!

As an adult, Dr. Melissa spent more than 20 years writing Dolly Doctor advice columns. She received — and answered — thousands of real-life letters from people like you! We've included some of them in this book and, yes, they're real too.

Unlike Dr. Melissa, I'm not an expert. But I do have a good memory, and I remember that even if you already know a ton about periods, getting your first one can be a bit daunting — maybe scary, maybe exciting, but always . . . *something*. So when it comes to periods, there's no such thing as a silly question. Regular, irregular, painful, painless, heavy, light — everyone's periods are different. So — WELCOME! This book will arm you with facts and rock-solid info so you can handle your period like a boss.

We hope it will help you feel confident as you get to know your body.

Let's go!

Yumi and Dr. Melissa

THE BASICS

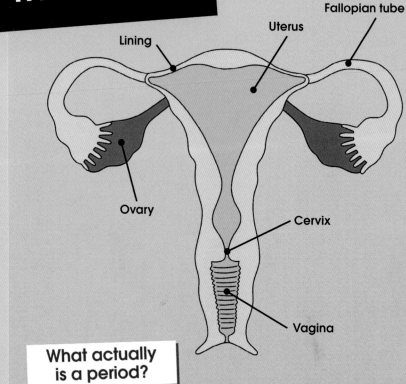

Fallopian tube

Uterus

Lining

Ovary

Cervix

Vagina

What actually is a period?

A *period* is a natural bleed that comes out of the vagina about once a month, usually lasting about five days. It is literally the shedding of the lining of your uterus — periodically. It's also known as *menstruation*.

It's as simple as that, and trust us, you will be able to handle it.

Who gets a period?

If you have a uterus, you will most likely get your period!

When is it coming?

Your first period occurs as part of puberty (for more on puberty, see page 122). Most people will get their periods between the ages of 10 and 15, but there is a wide range and some people will start even earlier or later.

Most of the time, there are some signs that your first period is coming. Turn to page 62 to learn more.

How long does it last?

The actual bleed

For most adolescents, the bleeding part lasts two to seven days, with an average of around five days.

The cycle

Your cycle is counted from the first day of your period (when you bleed) to the first day of your *next* period. It can take a couple of years for your cycle to find its own pattern. It's usually around 28–32 days, with variations from person to person and month to month. Teenagers can have even bigger variations (21–45 days). For more on your cycle, see page 148.

In life

Once you start getting your period, you tend to get it for the next 30 to 40 years, interrupted by pregnancy and childbirth (if you have kids), until menopause. Menopause is when your reproductive system shuts down and you can no longer make a baby in your body. The average age for a person to reach menopause is 51 years old.

QUESTIONS FOR DR. MELISSA

I'm scared!

66 I am a 12-year-old girl and I am terrified of getting my period. What do I do to calm myself down? 99

A lot of people feel scared about getting their period for the first time. If this is you, we promise *You are not the only one.* Of course it's OK to be scared. To you, it's an unknown. The best thing you can do when you're scared of something is to find out more about it. That means you're doing the right thing by reading this book!

Look around. Almost all the adult women you see in the world have experienced menstruation. And they have survived. And they have gone on to kick ass.

Take a deep breath. You are going to be OK!

MANAGING FEELINGS OF FEAR

1. Take deep breaths.
2. Know what it is you are fearful of.
3. Go for a walk.
4. Take a big drink of water.
5. Find someone to talk about it with.
6. Realize that you are not alone.

Does it hurt?

Probably not that much to begin with, especially for the first few months.

As you get older, period pain can become more common, although the feeling is different for everyone. If you do get some pain from your period, it can feel like heaviness, or a sort of muscle cramp behind where the elastic waistband of your underwear sits. Pain is not actually caused by the bleeding out of the vagina, but comes from muscle contractions of the uterus, which is higher up.

I didn't even notice my first period. It was completely painless and was just a few brown streaks on my underpants over about three days. It was actually my grandmother who told me, because she'd noticed it when she was doing the family's laundry! Some people might find that embarrassing, but for me it was easier talking to my grandma about it than anyone else. *Dr. Melissa*

If you're just starting out with your period or haven't had one yet, pain is probably not something you need to worry about right now. For more on period pain, see page 96.

As well as the flow of blood, I sometimes feel tenderness on my labia (or "outer lips"), as though I've got a bruise down there. The feeling lasts for about a day. Some of my friends get tummy cramps, or feel a bit achy below the belly button. *Yumi*

Why do you get periods?

AKA "Why the heck is blood lining my uterus when it never used to be there?!"

As you enter puberty, your body kicks off an amazing combination of hormone shifts and physical growth that causes your uterus to start growing a new lining of blood and other fluids. It's there to help a baby grow, and in the absence of pregnancy, your body wants to get rid of that lining, or "shed" it. Shedding is what we also describe as bleeding. It all has to do with the reproductive system, which you can learn more about on page 148.

Once you've had a period and the lining is gone for the month, your uterus starts accumulating a fresh lining all over again, which it will get rid of the next time around.

I think of it as an empty room. Starting in puberty, the walls, floor, and ceiling become lined with lovely red upholstery. Then we throw out the upholstery and start again. *Yumi*

How much blood comes out?

It may feel (and look) like a lot, but it isn't really — around four or five teaspoons over the first two to three days of bleeding. You can use pads, tampons, and other menstrual products to capture it — we've covered all your options on page 42.

These first few days are usually described as your "heaviest" days, because that's when the most fluid comes out (about 75–90 percent of the total blood loss). After that, the flow tapers off, becoming lighter and lighter until it stops. That really light flow at the end of your period leaves spots of blood on your underwear or on the pad, which is why it's sometimes called "spotting."

Where does my period come out of?

Your period comes out of your vagina, which is not the same as where your pee comes from. Your vagina is about three-quarters of an inch behind your urethra (your pee hole), and one inch in front of your anus (butt hole), but exact distances vary from body to body.

For more on your vagina, see page 120.

Why do periods come monthly? Is it because of the moon?

Although periods and full moons each come about once a month, the timing of the two seems to be just a coincidence. In adults, the average time from period to period is 28 days, but can be anywhere between 24 and 35 days. For young teens, it can be anywhere from 21 to 45 days. We call this a "cycle," and we count it from the first day of getting your period to the first day of your next one.

What does it look like?

When you first start getting your period, it is often brown or black in color, and sometimes just looks like streaks on your undies or pad. Once periods are established and more regular, the flow is usually a dark red during heavier days and can become brown as the period gets lighter. It varies from person to person, and period to period.

> I think I was confused because of the color. I was expecting a deep red, and it was more of a kind of browny color. I was like, "Is this it, or is it something else?" *Nevo, 22*

Which underwear is best to wear when you've got your period?

Wear what feels most comfortable for you! If you're wearing a pad, you might find that a wider gusset (the part that sits between your legs, under your vulva) is more supportive, like a boy-short brief. A thong probably isn't going to cut it!

Can anyone tell if I have my period?

NO ONE WILL KNOW THAT YOU HAVE YOUR PERIOD UNLESS YOU TELL THEM.

What will it feel like?

It feels like you have a small amount of wetness between your legs. But not *exactly* like you've wet your pants. For starters, what comes out is stickier than pee, and you also can't control the blood flow by tightening your pelvic floor muscles (the same muscles you use to stop and start peeing).

Having blood in your undies can get a bit messy, so most people wear a pad or use a tampon or menstrual cup when they have their period. If you're wearing a pad, the liquid will get absorbed so that you feel dry. If you are using a tampon or menstrual cup, you don't feel anything at all until they are full. See page 42 for more information about these menstrual products.

It's important to know that the flow of your period comes from your vagina, not your urethra (where urine comes from). When you have your period, you can sometimes feel a warm liquid coming out of your vagina, but it's a once-in-a-while type of sensation, not a constant stream.

Seeing blood in your undies for the first time can be a bit upsetting, but you'll get used to it! Even people who have been super squeamish about the sight of blood end up being pretty calm about their periods. *Yumi*

I'm a young disabled girl; I sometimes use a wheelchair and my dexterity isn't great. The level of your disability is going to make a difference in how it affects your period, but it doesn't have to be a catastrophe. Talking to young girls who are about to get their period and are disabled, I think: don't worry about it — it doesn't have to be a terrible thing and it doesn't have to be that hard. *Stella, 19*

Let me know if you want to chat about it more before it comes!

OMG, that would be great 😊

I'M WORRIED IT WILL NEVER COME

You might be feeling as though *all* your friends have their period, and yours will never show up. Or maybe you're hoping to be first! But if your period hasn't arrived yet, when should you start getting worried?

EVERY BODY IS DIFFERENT.

The short answer is: not for a while. If your period is still a no-show, you don't need to start thinking about talking to a doctor until you're 15 or 16 years old — and even then, things are likely to be fine. In the meantime, don't stress!

It might help put your mind at ease to ask your mom, sister, cousins, or older friends about when they first got their periods.

You may discover that theirs came later, in which case yours could come later too. Or you might find out that some of your family's periods started earlier, and some started later, which isn't that helpful! It's anyone's guess when yours will arrive, although you do get some clues from your own body — see page 62.

If you don't have a family member to ask, talk to someone at school — a trusted teacher, a school nurse, or a counselor. Try not to worry about being embarrassed — periods may seem scary or mortifying before they first start, but most adults with uteruses are used to getting them. After a few months, they don't seem like such a big deal anymore. (Before you know it, you will be offering advice to younger friends and family!)

I was almost 13 when I got my first period. I think my mom had been around the same age too, and it was the same for my younger sister. *Dr. Melissa*

BEFORE YOU GET YOUR PERIOD

Being prepared for something that's never happened to you before is tricky, right?

Luckily, there *are* some things you can do to prepare for your first period:

1. Put together your period pack.

Having your supplies on hand will help you feel ready for anything! To learn what goes into your period pack, see page 20.

2. Try on a pad.

Place the sticky side of the pad down onto your undies, underneath your vagina. Pull your undies up and then walk around. (Go to page 42 for more guidance.) How does it feel? Pat your behind — can you feel it? Put your outfit back on and take a look in the mirror — can you see the pad through your clothes? Probably not, right?

3. Buy black undies.

If you'd rather not see the inevitable leaks and spills, black undies are a good investment because they are darker than blood and mask stains. We recommend phasing in *lots* of black ones — you might feel more comfortable wearing these on heavier days.

4. Talk about it!

Ask your friends and the other period bosses in your life about their periods. We totally understand feeling a bit shy about it, but from experience we figure you can always find a couple of menstruating adults who are up for a period chat! They may be able to share their experiences and give you some basic advice.

5. Read a book!

The best thing about novels is that they allow you to experience something before it happens to you. Here are some of our favorite books that actually deal with periods in a meaningful way:

 Revenge of the Red Club
by Kim Harrington

Are You There God? It's Me, Margaret.
by Judy Blume

 To Night Owl From Dogfish
by Holly Goldberg Sloan
and Meg Wolitzer

AND, OF COURSE, READ THIS BOOK! KNOWLEDGE IS POWER.

I talked to two of my cousins and to my best friend. They knew a ton about periods from their mothers, ages before they got them, and shared that with me. We still collectively freaked out before any of us got our first period, but once we did, it was like, "Oh! That's not so bad after all." *Dr. Meliara*

BE PREPARED WITH A PERIOD PACK

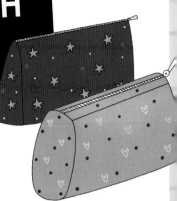

One thing that will help you feel ready for your period is having a *period pack* in your bag!

A period pack is a small zipped-up bag of everything you need for your period. It comes with you everywhere so you don't get stuck somewhere with no supplies. A small pencil case or pouch is the perfect size — something that doesn't take up much room, and that you feel comfortable pulling out of your backpack, schoolbag, or purse when you need it.

This is one of the reasons many adult ladies carry handbags. Handbags are basically glorified period packs. *Yumi*

My daughter got hers at 12 years old. At her school you have to go to the bathroom in pairs, so she was with a friend. She sat down on the toilet and saw a little bit of blood on her undies, and shouted out, "I think I got my period!" Her friend went, "Right, I'll go get supplies." She went to her bag, gathered up a few other friends, and they all grabbed their period stashes and came back and gave her the options. *Cymone, 45*

Your period pack should include:

Menstrual products

Whether you prefer pads or tampons, include three in your pack. If you're not sure yet, pads are a good place to start, but it's also nice to keep a spare tampon in there. They don't take up much space, and one of your friends — or a stranger — might ask you for one. (It always feels good to help out in a period emergency!) To learn more about your options and how to use pads, tampons, and more, see page 42.

Spare undies

It's a good idea to keep these in a plastic baggie. If you have a period bleed on your undies, you can swap them for the clean pair and pop the stained ones into the empty bag to be washed when you get home.

> I bring a small bag to carry pads, tampons, and panty liners. OH MY GOSH, I only recently learned to put spare undies in there! If it's your first, second, or third day of your period, always put spare undies in there. If it's your fourth day, don't bother. *Tans, 13*

Depending on how you feel when you get your period, you may add the following:

Pain medication

If you sometimes take pain medication like ibuprofen or acetaminophen for your period, add some tablets to your period pack.

Emergency chocolate

Just in case, because chocolate is yummy.

Keep your period pack handy so you can easily grab it at school, on your way home, out with friends, or at your after-school job. A special little bag might seem a bit fancy or fussy, but we *strongly recommend* it because your period supplies can get really beaten up if they're bouncing around loose inside your schoolbag. Or they might jump out of your bag when you're not looking!

I used to host a live TV show where a *lot* could go wrong — so to make myself feel more secure, I would wear two pairs of underpants! It made me feel more in control. A good period pack should make you feel the same way. Protected. Secure. Like, babe, I've got this! *Yumi*

I'm a big fan of the roller coaster of emotions you experience when your period surprises you ("Oh no!"), but then you remember you're prepared ("Oh yes!"). Possibly the only better feeling is when you're in a bathroom and a stranger asks you for a tampon or a pad, and you can swoop in to save their day. *Penny, 33*

What about at home?

What's the home version of a period pack? Good question! It's somewhere handy you can stash all your supplies, like in your bathroom or bedroom. If you live with someone else who gets her period, suss out what she does and go along with that.

You can either keep your supplies all together in a small bag or just put the packages of pads or tampons somewhere within reach. The closer to the toilet, the easier it will be to get them when your period arrives — so you can either leave them out nearby or, if you prefer, just in the nearest cabinet.

BAGS

TRASH

In my house, I keep a couple of pads and tampons by the toilet at all times. I don't put them away in the cupboard — they're just out there in the open where everyone can see them. No one minds. Getting your period is normal!

And since menstrual products should never be flushed down the toilet, I also make sure there's a trash can next to the toilet. That way no one has to take their used pad or tampon any farther than a few feet from the toilet. *Yumi*

Dealing With Your First Period

Wow! OK. So after all the buildup, it actually happened! You sat down to use the toilet, discovered something red or brown in your undies, and now you've got your period. Congratulations!

So what do you do now?

I was at home, sitting on the toilet, and then blood came out. I was like, *Uuuuuuhm, WHAT IS THIS?* I freaked out and asked my mom. I think I was in seventh grade, and I had *no idea* about periods. I was not expecting it. None of my friends had really talked about it. I did have a couple of friends who had gotten their periods before me, but it was a cultural thing that we didn't really talk about it — it was a very private, very personal thing. *Hsin-Ju, 34*

Find a pad

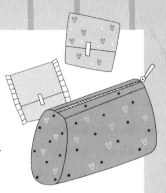

If you're lucky, you'll have your period pack ready to go in your bag, no matter where you are (although if you're really, *really* lucky, you'll be at home). Take out a pad, unwrap it, stick it on your undies, and then feel like you have a special secret for the rest of the day.

Or you might like to tell some friends about it, and you can all make a fuss over this exciting milestone!

A few hours later, you'll need to change the pad by taking out the old one, wrapping it in toilet paper or the wrapper of a new pad, putting it in a trash can or sanitary disposal unit, and then putting the new pad in your underpants.

If you don't have your period pack with you, fold up some toilet paper and tuck that into your undies instead. If your undies are snug, it should be fine for a little while; it's not as absorbent as a pad. Then tell a friend, a teacher, or a trusted adult, and they should be able to help you out with some pads until you get home.

> It was nighttime, and I went to the bathroom and found that I had just gotten my period. I was confused about what to do next. My mom was out, but my older sister helped me with a pad. My older sister gives me so much help with things like managing cramps, stains, and feeling sick. *Chloe, 16*

Tell the people at home!

So, now that it's here, it's a good idea to tell someone, even if it feels awkward. Be brave! Your mom, dad, older sister, or main caregiver will want to know, as they'll be the ones helping you buy pads, tampons, cups, or period undies in the future. And also, this is *good* news. You're growing up! Your body is doing the things it's meant to do! Chances are they'll be super glad for you.

Smile to yourself

Your period came! Look at yourself in the mirror. Who is this amazing person looking back and taking more steps toward becoming a grown-up?

You're not alone if your first period is a bit anticlimactic! My first couple of periods weren't even red — they were a murky sort of brown and a bit watery. I was hoping it'd be more like a murder scene and instead it was like Shrek's swamp. *Yumi*

I was in seventh grade and discovered it when I went to the bathroom after school. I called my mom at work, and she was like, "OH MY GOD, THAT'S SO EXCITING!" Then she called out to her entire office and shouted, "My daughter's got her period!" Deeply, deeply embarrassing. I was fine for Mom to know, but I didn't expect the whole world to know! *Audrey, 37*

I remember when I first got my period, I just walked into my sister's room, grabbed a tampon, and did what I had to do! Then I walked downstairs and said to my mom, "I got my period," and she asked if I had something to take care of it. I said, "Yeah, I got a tampon out of Danielle's room," and then my sister got angry with me for going into her room without asking! *Nicole, 40*

All my friends started getting it and I was kind of late compared to them so I thought I was really ready for it, but it was still a shock and really overwhelming! Straight-away I went to my mom, and I was really nervous to tell her — I don't know why — and I said, "Mom, I think I got my period!" And she was like, "That's wonderful!" And I was like, "No, it's not!" *Kiara, 15*

WAYS TO SHARE THE NEWS

Hey, Mom, guess what? I failed English! Just kidding, I got my period.

Gran, can you come in here and have a look at this?

Dad, I got my period!

Hey, Dad, we'll have to start buying pads for a while. I mean, forever.

Hey, bestie, I got my period for the first time!

30

YOU GOT IT!

Celebrate With a Period Party!

Getting your period for the first time is a huge milestone, and it only happens once. So you might feel like seizing the moment and celebrating!

Whether you're throwing the period party for yourself, your best friend, or a sibling, here are some great ideas to welcome the very first period:

Hang out with your friends and make mugs of ginger tea and mini sandwiches, and talk about the first time *they* got their periods. Then maybe settle down to marathon your favorite show together.

Tie red and white balloons to the front fence. No one has to know why, but the red is for blood and the white is for the pads you use to manage the blood. It can be like a secret joke or a big, loud announcement.

PERIOD PARTY

You might really want to get into the theme by serving red food, like red velvet cake!

Have a party where you invite relatives, like aunties, cousins, and sisters. If you want, they can all talk about the first time they got their period, or you can just get on with the important business of making one another laugh.

We were very open about periods — we actually threw little parties for each other! We basically just got each other presents. I remember when I got mine, I got a pair of Kookai underpants that were sort of like boxers — which I really liked because they were sort of androgynous — and a sudoku book. *Nevo, 22*

You might prefer not to celebrate, and that's perfectly fine too. Why not curl up with a good book and not budge until you want to?

My mom was really excited and I think she said something like, "That's fantastic!" and gave me a hug. And then she got a pad for me and showed me how to use it. I think my mom made it a little bit of a low-key celebration between her and me. She let me know that it was something positive and lovely and important.

I definitely would follow a similar attitude as my mom and probably build on that from a traditional perspective as well. Because we lost a lot of our traditional Wiradjuri culture, we'd want to keep this perspective of celebration and that it's a very important milestone in a woman's life. I can imagine that it could be so many things, but if it's framed in the right way, it's very empowering.

Samantha, 30

34

I was 13 when I got my period for the first time. As my underwear got dirty, I showed it to my mother and confirmed it. As a custom of Japan, we celebrated by cooking red rice (sticky rice with red beans in it), like it was a birthday. *Itsuko*, 55

If you feel comfortable, have a regular party with all your friends (gender = irrelevant) and sing "happy birthday" to your period. Everyone can bring gift-wrapped pads, tampons, period undies, or menstrual cups!

I told my mom — she was really happy and took me out for dinner with my godmother. They sat there for hours and told stories about getting their periods and *that was even worse* than getting my period! I found it really embarrassing to have to talk about those things! *Marisa*, 33

I CAN'T TALK ABOUT PERIODS WITH MY PARENTS

Talking about your period for the first time can be nerve-racking, especially if you feel shy or embarrassed (which is totally normal — it's new!). But what happens if you try to raise the subject with your parents or caregivers at home, yet they just don't seem to want to talk about it?

Reasons might be:

* They don't want you to grow up.

* They literally don't know what to say.

* They're always working.

* They're always on their phone.

* They're embarrassed or shy when it comes to talking about periods.

* It hasn't occurred to them that you might have reached that stage in your life.

* Your mom, dad, or caregiver has problems of their own that make it harder for them to focus on yours.

* There's a language barrier.

Whatever the reason your parents or caregivers are tricky to communicate with, it's not your fault. When we were writing this book, we spoke to a lot of people who had parents who weren't great communicators on this topic — and they survived.

The fact that you have this book in your hands is a good sign. It means that the person who gave you this book cares, or that *you* care and are smart enough to seek out information and find solutions.

Dad, I need to talk to you about my period. I know it makes you uncomfortable—but this really needs to happen.

Mom, can we schedule some time to talk about the fact that I'll be getting my period soon, soon?

Mom. Mom, Mom, Mom, Mom. Listen. Periods. Me. Talk. Let's.

Here are some ways to start the conversation about periods at home:

You could write a note, send a calendar invitation via computer, or send a text.

We think it's really important to have at least *one* person you can talk to about your period, so if it isn't going to be a parent, the first place to look is your wider family — aunts, sisters, trusted friends — and then your school. There will almost always be someone at school you can talk to about awkward stuff — and it's often someone who has had special training in how to have those conversations! Ask to see the guidance counselor, the school psychologist, a female PE teacher, health teacher, or just that teacher who's always had your back.

Beyond school, there are these fantastic people who know all about the human body — doctors and nurses!

THINK ABOUT THE BEST WAY TO GET THROUGH TO YOUR MOM OR DAD, AND USE THAT METHOD OF COMMUNICATION TO START THE CONVERSATION.

1 NEW TXT

Maybe you have a regular doctor or you're familiar with a medical practice (aka doctor's office) that you've visited a few times? Doctors aren't just there for when you get sick or injured — they also know about puberty and all its changes, and it's fine to visit them just to have a chat about these things.

If none of these work, you can try an organization like Planned Parenthood.

I'm here to help!

There were always some girls in my friendship group who were more comfortable saying if they had their period or if they had cramps. It wasn't until we were about 16 that it became more common to talk about it. We never talked about the details of our periods, or how our experiences differed from one another. It was always just that we had it — and the rest was quite veiled. *Amelia,* 33

WHAT HAPPENS AFTER YOUR FIRST PERIOD?

Nothing much! You deal with it, and life goes on as normal. No one looks at you like you're special, because no one can tell anything is different unless you say something or have a period party.

Every month you will need to make sure your bathroom cabinet is stocked with period supplies. And don't worry if your periods aren't regular to begin with — they tend to settle into a predictable pattern after a year or so.

A lot of girls get their first period and then it doesn't happen again for a few months. This happened to me. I got a couple of weird periods about a month apart, then nothing for a couple of months, and then it came a few more times, then nothing, and then it started to be pretty regular after that. *Yumi*

My second period came about four months after my first one. I began to wonder if the first one had been a dream. My cycle got regular only after about eight months. *Dr. Melissa*

When I told my older sisters, they were like, "Whoo-hoo! You're a woman now, you're one of us!" *Nadine, 35*

I think because of all the hoo-ha around the first time you get your period, I actually expected that I would wake up the next morning and be an accomplished woman! *Marihuzka, 36*

Basically, in traditional Indonesian culture (which is how my mom grew up), when a girl gets her period, it's seen as a total transition into womanhood. Indonesian culture views having your period as powerful because you are now literally able to give life. There are so many customs that go along with having your period, like you can't visit any ancient temples while you're on your period, or any places of sacred significance. This is because the energy is too powerful. They believe that blood energy belongs to the earth and that sacred sites such as temples have sky energy — and the two are not to be muddled. (Wild, I know!) *Amandah, 30*

HOW TO MANAGE YOUR PERIOD

Pads, Tampons, and More

There are lots of things you can use to manage your period like a boss. They're collectively referred to as *menstrual products* or *sanitary items*. Here are the most common ones and how to use them!

YOU CAN BUY TAMPONS AND PADS FROM SUPERMARKETS, PHARMACIES, AND MOST CONVENIENCE STORES.

Pads

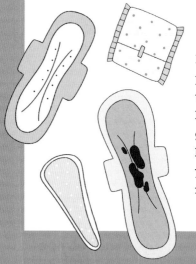

Pads are easy to use, and you'll probably find them the best product to start with when you're new to having your period. (They're pretty good the rest of the time too.) Pads have an adhesive strip that sticks to your undies, and they absorb period flow as it comes out of the vagina.

To use a pad, you just peel off the protective layer or wrapping, then press the sticky side onto the inside middle of your undies, underneath where your vagina sits. Once the pad is stuck down, pull up your undies and see how it feels.

Occasionally pads can leak (like if you have a heavy flow or you go too long without changing them). If there's going to be leakage, it's more likely to come from the back than the front, so try to put a little extra pad toward your butt.

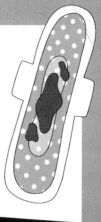

Pads come in a few different lengths and thicknesses, so you might need to try a few sizes, shapes, and brands until you find something you're comfortable with. Liners are similar to pads and are for catching a very light flow or discharge, or for "just in case" days.

My friend Lila prefers to use pads because it lets her see what's going on. She has a better idea of what is coming out of her body. *Yumi*

wings Some pads come with "wings," which wrap around underneath your undies. This is to stop your undies from getting reddish-brown marks on the sides if the pad bunches up a little when you walk around. It's up to you whether you want to use pads with wings or not.

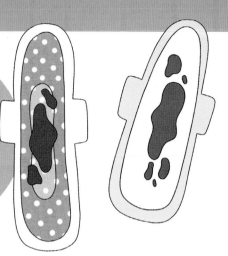

> THE USEFUL THING ABOUT PADS IS THAT WHEN YOU GO TO THE BATHROOM, YOU'LL BE ABLE TO SEE WHETHER YOUR PAD NEEDS CHANGING.

A few dots or swipes of blood are OK to ignore. But if the pad is heavy with blood, it's time to swap a fresh one in.

If you have a physical disability that restricts your movement, you might find pads are the easiest things to use.

You can also buy reusable pads — see page 117 for more information on those.

> For my first-ever cycle, I was changing my pad every one to two hours because I was so conscious of the bleeding. I used up the whole package of pads that day! It wasn't until later that I realized a package was meant to last much longer. There were other women in the house and the pads were supposed to be for all of us, but because I was changing them so regularly, I had used them all up! *Hawiine, 23*

WHERE DO I PUT USED PADS AND TAMPONS?

Don't flush them down the toilet, as they can block the pipes. Instead, wrap them in toilet paper and put them in the nearest trash can. You should put their wrappers in the trash can too.

Most women's bathrooms contain sanitary disposal bins for this purpose. If there are no bins anywhere in sight, just wrap your used pad or tampon in toilet paper and tuck it into your bag or pocket to throw out as soon as you see a trash can.

45

Tampons absorb period flow from inside the vagina, which involves putting them in (and pulling them out again when they're full). You only use one tampon at a time.

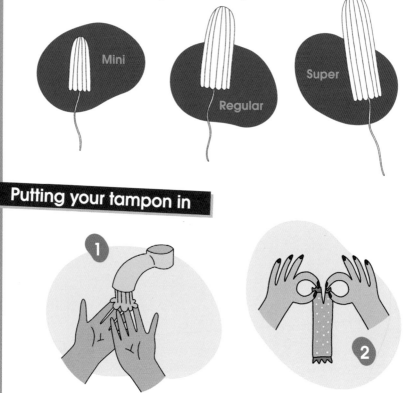

Mini

Regular

Super

Putting your tampon in

First, wash your hands thoroughly, then remove the tampon from its wrapper. You'll see a bit of string curled up at one end; loosen it before you insert the tampon.

Then push the tampon up inside your vagina, leaving the string dangling out so you can pull it out later. If it's inserted correctly, the tampon doesn't hurt going in and you can't feel it once it's in there. Breathing slowly can help keep you calm and relax the muscles around your vagina to make insertion easier.

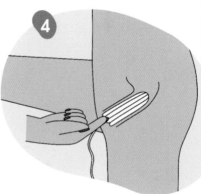

Some tampons come with an applicator. Instead of inserting the tampon with your finger, you insert the applicator and push the narrower part into the wider part, which slides the tampon up into your vagina. Then you remove the applicator and throw it away.

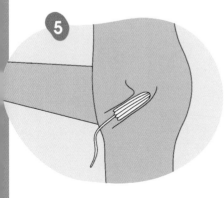

Using any kind of tampon means there won't be a bulge in your underwear, which can be good for ballet and gymnastics, and it also means you can go swimming without getting waterlogged.

Taking your tampon out

After three to six hours, wash your hands well and then remove the tampon by finding the string. Then just pull on the string and the tampon should come out easily. If the string isn't dangling down, that's OK — you'll need to feel around until you find it.

Remember to pull down *and* forward, toward your front — if you pull straight down, the tampon can bump against the back wall of the vagina and feel stuck.

The more you use tampons, the easier you'll find it is to tell when it's time to change them. A good trick is to tug gently on the string; when the tampon is heavy with blood, it will come out smoothly. If it's still a bit dry, it might be a little stiffer and "grippy," but it will still come out — or you can leave it in for a little bit longer. However, you should never leave a tampon in for longer than eight hours. If you use them overnight, be sure to put in a new one right before bed.

The heavier your flow, the more often you'll need to change your tampon. Different tampons have different absorbency levels, ranging from "mini" (for light periods) to "super" (for heavy periods).

TIP

Practicing with tampons in between periods or on light period days can be really useful.

TIP

A gentle start can be to practice with mini-tampons, using a bit of lubricant to help the tampon glide in. You can buy lubricant from the supermarket, in the "personal care" aisle.

It's always interesting to see how much blood the tampon has absorbed. Sometimes a used tampon is dark red and utterly soaked through. Other times it is still mostly white.

On a hectic day, I might use a tampon *and* a pad at the same time, for the extra level of absorbency—particularly on the first two days of bleeding. *Yumi*

Having trouble?

A common problem is putting the tampon straight up, so that it hits the front wall of the vagina and won't go farther. If you tilt the tampon back toward your spine, it will go in easier.

TIP

Our research shows that finding a friend IRL to show you the angle to insert a tampon can make all the difference. You don't have to get nude; they'll just show you over your clothes.

The tampon should go in as far as you can push it (it can't get past your cervix, so you can't possibly lose it), about as far as your second knuckle or, for some, the whole finger-length.

Once it's sitting at the top of the vagina (against the opening of the cervix), you should not be able to feel it inside you when you're walking, running, sitting, or lying down. In fact, you might forget it's there! Until it becomes soaked with period blood, and then you might feel a kind of heaviness, or some blood might leak out.

Always remember to free the string of the tampon and have it hanging out when you insert it. If the string isn't dangling down, just feel around until you find it.

Using tampons is like learning to ride a bike. It usually takes some practice, but once you get there, it's super easy and you'll never *not* be able to do it again! Even so, the first few times can be . . . an experience. Here's what I remember about my early tampon-trouble times:

"Why doesn't it fit?!"   "Help! Where's the string???"
"Owwww!"   "This is ridiculous! Why is
"Oh no, it's stuck."   it soooo difficult????"

But I kept practicing and I figured it out pretty quickly after that! *Dr. Melissa*

Get to know your vagina

One of the reasons it can feel weird and difficult to get a tampon in is that you might not be used to feeling the inside of your vagina. A simple tip is to put a clean finger inside your vagina and see how far you can reach up inside. *(It is your body, and you are totally allowed to do this.)* Get to know the inside of your vagina and how it slopes upward and back. See page 120 for more about the vagina.

Period panties

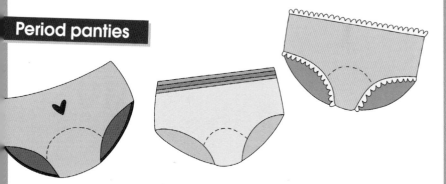

Period panties are underpants with a cloth pad built into the crotch area (the part where your vagina sits). They come in lots of different sizes, absorbencies, and styles. The best thing about them is that they can be reused — you just rinse them, put them in the washing machine, and dry them so they're ready for next time!

Period panties are fantastic for people who don't want to use disposable menstrual products. They are also great for people who aren't near stores and can't just run out for a package of pads.

Depending on your flow, period panties are amazing from about day three of your period, when the flow is usually lighter. Using them feels like you don't even have a period! If you have a heavy flow on days one and two, you might like to use them in combination with something else, like a tampon.

If you're still getting used to your period and you're trying period panties for the first time, consider using backup in the form of an extra pad, a tampon, or some extra undies over the top.

Period panties can be bought easily online and are stocked in superstores and department stores. They're more expensive upfront than pads and tampons — prices vary from $15 to around $35–$50 a pair — but they're much cheaper in the long run.

Tips for using period panties

1. Rinse them in cold water as soon as you're done with them. Give them a rinse in the sink or shower as soon as you take them off. It only takes a few seconds, and then they're dealt with immediately. Trust us, you don't want your used period panties drying out and going hard and crusty in the corner of your bedroom!

2. **Wash them in cold water.**
Once they've been rinsed, they can go in the regular laundry (with other dark or colored clothes is best) — just make sure it's a cold wash cycle, as heat makes blood congeal.

3. **Let them dry.** Period panties take longer to dry than regular undies, so if you want to use them as your main method, you will need at least four to six pairs, and you'll need to wash them regularly.

4. **They love sunshine.** It's best to dry them in the sun, not the dryer. If you can't hang them outside, inside is fine — just make sure you give them time to get completely dry before you put them away or use them again.

OTHER USES

Period panties are also popular for people who sweat a lot, or who have leaky bladders (this can sometimes happen to people who've had babies). Period panties just wick the moisture away!

53

Menstrual cups

A menstrual cup (or moon cup) is a small silicone cup that you fold over twice and then push up inside your vagina, usually using two fingers. It springs open to its original cup shape once it's inside and catches the blood leaving your uterus.

Menstrual cups are a cheaper and more environmentally friendly way of managing menstruation, as you can reuse them easily — just wash and go! Most pharmacies sell them, or you can buy them online.

You can use cups for up to 12 hours at a time, making them absolutely amazing if you're hopeless at remembering to bring pads to school, or for long trips or work shifts. They're also great if you don't have much money, as one cup — while initially expensive — can last around ten years.

They come in many sizes and can be tricky to get the hang of. As with tampons, they take practice, and it's safe to practice in between periods.

$1^1/_2$–$1^3/_4$"

$1^3/_4$–$2^1/_4$"

$2/_5$–$3/_4$"

The bottom of the cup has a stem just like the stem of a wineglass (without the base). Contrary to popular belief, you do *not* pull on the stem to remove the cup. We'll get to that in a sec!

Putting it in

The best way to insert the cup is with a wet cup and dry hands. (The wet cup will slide in more easily and the dry fingers will grip it better.)

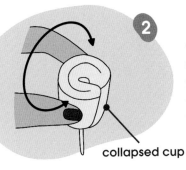

Collapse the cup by flattening it using your fingers, then folding it in half to make it smaller — slightly bigger than a tampon.

collapsed cup

Holding it in this squashed-down shape, lift your leg and insert the cup into your vagina.

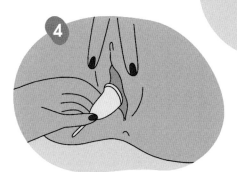

It's handy to remember at this point that it does *not* go in as far as a tampon!

The base of the cup should sit about half an inch up from the vaginal opening. Do not aim the cup straight up. It should be pointing toward your spine at a 45-degree angle. (If it's too high, it will feel uncomfortable.)

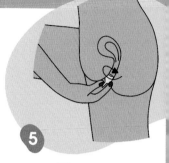

When the cup is in place, allow it to spring open. Many people report that they can feel the "pop" of it opening. You can adjust it quite easily using your thumb or fingers.

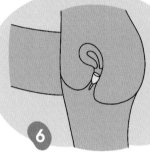

Run your finger around the cup to feel that there are no crunched-up sides. It should be open and smooth, forming a sort of suction seal around the wall of your vagina. If it's inserted correctly, it shouldn't feel weird or noticeable when you're walking or sitting or doing any other activity. (See page 120 for more on the vagina.)

TIP

If it seems to be sitting well but there is still some of the stem poking out of your vagina, it means the stem is too long for you. Next time you have it out, use scissors to trim a little length off the end of the stem. (Not too much! You can always cut it back more if you need to.) The cups are designed this way and needing to trim the stem is common.

Taking it out

When removing the cup, it's important to make sure your hands are clean and dry. You might also like to do it over the toilet or in the shower, as a small gush of blood can come out.

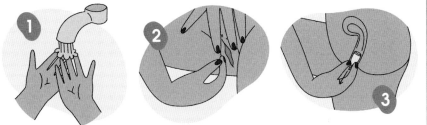

First, use the stem as a guide for your fingers to find the top of the cup. Squeeze gently on the cup as close to the rim as possible to break the seal of air that has probably formed. (Squeezing the cup will prevent an air vacuum forming that will make it harder to pull the cup out.) Once you have done this, pull the menstrual cup out. There might be some spillage.

The cup will have filled with menstrual fluid, which you rinse out first in cold water. Then wash the cup well with warm, soapy water, and rinse again in cold water. Your menstrual cup is ready to reuse.

A menstrual cup that has been collapsed ready for insertion is still bigger than a tampon, so if tampons seem too big and freak you out a bit, you're probably not ready to try a cup yet.

People say to me, "Menstrual cups changed my life!" and "Why didn't I try these sooner?" I love my menstrual cup. I love pulling it out in the shower and getting to see what has come out of my body. It demystifies the whole period process and makes me feel more in tune with my cycle. *Yumi*

KEEPING TRACK OF YOUR PERIOD

To know what's going on with your body, it's really handy to keep track of when you bleed — even though it might take a few months or years for your cycle to become more regular.

You can easily track your period with your school planner or home calendar — start by adding a little red circle on the first day of your flow. (If you have a year-to-a-page in your planner, this could be even easier — then you can see your cycle at a glance.)

The longer you track, the easier you'll find it is to predict when your next period might come. You may have heard that a "monthly" menstrual cycle is 28 days long, but this is just an average — it varies from person to person and can be up to 45 days long for teens. The cycle is counted from the first day of bleeding to the first day of your next period. See page 148 for more on the monthly hormone cycle.

If you like, you can also take note of the length of your period, your moods, discharge, and any pain symptoms. Knowing where your grumpy days sit in your cycle can help predict when

My hair gets greasy and I feel super angry with my dad about four days out. *Max, 13*

58

I always get a pimple on my chin two or three days before my period is about to start. *Amy, 13*

On the first day of my period, I usually write the letter *P* (for period) in a big circle on the calendar that we keep on the fridge. And my family draws an angry face on the day when my PMS symptoms are the worst! This helps me predict when my next period will be and when my next grumpy day will be. *Yumi*

your period is coming too. (See page 92 for more on PMS.) If you want to get super detailed, you can also make notes about cravings, how you sleep, and your energy levels. You might notice lots of changes during this time, or you might notice nothing different at all! It depends on the person.

If you have a smartphone, there is a wide variety of excellent and free apps that make tracking your period and symptoms easy, and even kind of fun (see page 159)!

The first time came as a surprise. I was 13, turning 14. It was weird — like I didn't really have a cycle — I had it a week on, a week off for, like, six weeks. And then I had it two weeks off, one week on for about three or four weeks, then it went three weeks off, one week on, four weeks off, one week on, five weeks off, one week on — and it's never really gotten better. Now it's — I dunno, I get one week in between and it's really light and it just comes out of nowhere and there's no schedule at all! *Kiara, 15*

We know many people feel scared about getting their first period. Answering the many letters to Dolly Doctor about periods reminded me how much worry is out there. But there was also a really lovely curiosity about this mysterious "thing" that was about to happen. We've put together some of the most frequently asked questions about periods and other fun facts to help describe the body's incredible natural processes. *Dr. Melissa*

QUESTIONS FOR DR. MELISSA

Discharge!

66 When I went to the bathroom the other night, I had all this gooey stuff on my underpants. It was clear and white. What is that stuff? Does it mean I am going to get my period? 99

Discharge is totally normal and nothing to be alarmed about. As your body develops, the cervix (the opening of the uterus) is making mucus and the vagina is becoming more moist. This causes a noticeable flow of fluid to come out and end up on your undies. Some kids call this a "snail trail." This discharge, or *secretion*, appears clear or white, and sometimes dries yellow in your undies.

There's no need to freak out about it. This "goo" is natural, normal, and will appear at some point early in puberty. It's just part of your body kicking into gear for menstruation, sex, and reproduction. If it bothers you, you can always use a liner to keep the discharge off your undies.

Discharge is a sign that

I find it really interesting that no one ever wants to talk about discharge! Why? It's not discussed much in school sex ed, and a lot of people seem to pretend it doesn't exist! One reason might be because discharge is sometimes connected to sexy feelings. Meaning, sometimes if you're having romantic or sexy thoughts, you'll notice more discharge flow connected to these thoughts. It can also just flow for no apparent reason! *Yumi*

everything is going well in your body. The only time you need to worry about it is if it seems to be coming out in copious amounts, has a really strong odor, and/or accompanies itching. A light odor is totally normal. If you think something is wrong with your discharge, go and see your doctor or show an older female friend.

There were SO many questions to Dolly Doctor about discharge in the lead-up to the first period! It seemed to freak a lot of people out. It's like everyone is taught, "OK, here are your boobs, your pubes, and your period. But don't mention the discharge!" *Dr. Melissa*

The rest of my body is changing. Does this mean my period is coming?

❝ I am 13 but I still don't have my period. Are there any signs to show me when I am getting it? ❞

Doctors and scientists look for a few signs to predict when your period is coming. Developing breasts is the earliest sign, closely followed by pubic hair. It varies, but the first period comes on average two years after your breasts start to develop.

In the months leading up to the first period, you might notice clear fluid coming out of your vagina ("secretions," or "discharge"). Once vaginal secretions become regular over months or even a year or so, it's a good sign that your periods are on their way soon.

Poop

It's natural to poop more when you're having a period! During the first couple of days of your period, your body releases a hormone called prostaglandin, which does a bunch of things, including getting your uterus to contract to help squeeze out the period blood. (Picture it like an invisible hand squeezing a stress ball.)

This hormone can also work on your intestines, squeezing them and making some of us poop a lot during the first couple of days!

I remember the first time there was a clot — thinking that there was something wrong and not asking anyone about it, just waiting and seeing. I seemed to still be alive a few weeks later, so I figured it was OK! I had never seen anything written about clotting and I didn't know it was a thing. But you can really feel it, particularly when you're wearing a pad. (Blood? Of course clotting!) *Amelia,* 33

Is a blood clot also my period?

66 Sometimes during my period I feel like a gush of blood comes out. But when I have a look, it turns out to be like a small lump of blood clot. So what is it exactly? 99

Period blood can be dark red and a thick fluid, or it can be brown and have small bits of tissue (those lining cells) or blood clots, jelly-like blobs of blood. These are nothing to worry about.

Your uterus is simply shedding whatever's in there that it doesn't need this time around. Pretty clever, hey?

FACT: The lining of the uterus that sheds (i.e., your period) is a combination of blood, fluid from the cervix and vagina called "secretions," and special cells from the lining of the uterus. That's why period "blood" looks different from the blood that you see if, say, you cut your finger.

PERIOD *Challenges*

Handling your period like a boss can take some practice! Here are some common challenges and how you can sail right through them.

What's the worst that can happen?

Once you get your head around the *worst* that can happen with your period on an ordinary day, you can relax! Because the very worst thing isn't that bad. It won't kill you, or hurt any of the people you care deeply about — it might be a bit embarrassing, but you'll get through it. You might even find it funny when it's over.

Leaks

The worst that can happen is that your period spills out from your underwear and leaks onto your clothes or bedding. Maybe other people will notice,

Yep, it happened to me. So embarrassing. I was 15. I survived. I even laughed about it later. *Dr. Melissa*

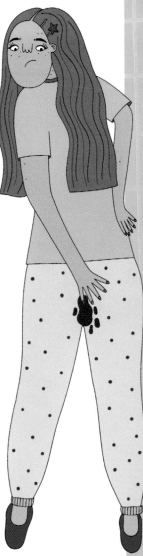

I find that if I'm feeling really embarrassed (or worried, or upset) and I have to talk to someone, it helps to start by saying, "Hey, I'm really embarrassed/worried/upset about this, so please don't laugh/make me feel worse . . ." Being upfront about our feelings is a great way to deal with sticky situations, and, well, life in general. *Dr. Melissa*

maybe not. Maybe you'll feel mortified, but you'll put in a fresh pad, tie a sweatshirt around your waist, and get on with life.

If you're unlucky, you might bleed onto the car upholstery, the bus seat, your wheelchair, or someone's couch. If that happens, you'll do your best to wipe it off, and maybe you'll feel bad for a short time — but it's not a big deal. It might even seem funny.

If you're surprised by a leak, stay calm. Depending on where you are, you might feel OK to just casually get up and find a bathroom where you can deal with the leak. Leaks onto dark clothes or thicker fabrics, like denim, aren't going to be so obvious. In fact, they may not be noticeable at all. You might be able to wait until you get home to deal with it. It might be a small enough leak that you can sponge it off with cold water.

If you're nowhere near a bathroom, or if you're wearing light-colored clothes, your best bet is to put something around your butt. If necessary, call for help. A friend, your mom or sister — anyone nearby who can lend you their jacket to tie around your waist. Sweaters, bags, scarves, and spare clothing can also work. Challenges like this can make us very creative!

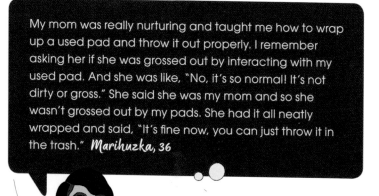

My mom was really nurturing and taught me how to wrap up a used pad and throw it out properly. I remember asking her if she was grossed out by interacting with my used pad. And she was like, "No, it's so normal! It's not dirty or gross." She said she was my mom and so she wasn't grossed out by my pads. She had it all neatly wrapped and said, "It's fine now, you can just throw it in the trash." *Marihuzka, 36*

Smells

Because your pad is close to your body and warm from your body heat, you may be able to smell it when you go to the bathroom and pull down your underpants. But don't worry about other people smelling it the rest of the time. When the pad is locked away inside your underwear, there isn't such a strong odor — and everyone else is farther away from the source than you!

Even so, the worst that can happen is that you forget to shower one day and have a bit of a period odor that other people can smell. So you'll go home and take a shower. No big deal.

In all my life, I have never smelled anyone's period blood but my own. *Yumi* (who has an excellent sense of smell)

TO MANAGE SMELLS, CHANGE YOUR UNDERWEAR EVERY DAY AND SHOWER ONCE A DAY AND YOU SHOULD BE FINE.

67

Having your period is nothing to be ashamed about. Neither is carrying pads or tampons or your period pack. So you shouldn't be ashamed if a pad or tampon falls out of your bag in front of other people. All that will happen is that other people will know that you get your period sometimes, and so what? So does half the population. And if some tries to shame you, know that they are doing it out of ignorance. Find a friend or trusted adult to talk it through with.

PART OF GROWING UP IS PERFECTING YOUR SHRUG.

Stuck

What if a tampon gets stuck and you can't get it out?

First off, don't stress out — this isn't the end of the world! This sometimes happens to people, so you're not the only one.

Now, let me reassure you: a tampon *cannot get lost* in your vagina — it has nowhere to go but out, so eventually it WILL come out, one way or another.

The best thing to do is wash your hands and then insert a clean finger (or two fingers) to try to pull it out yourself. Take the time to do it calmly in a place where you feel safe. The shower or bathroom, for instance, where you know you probably won't be interrupted, and where you can safely try. Don't use any other tools to try to get it out — this could be dangerous.

If you've tried your best to get the tampon out and you definitely can't, you will have to go to your doctor — or a family planning clinic if there's one nearby — where a doctor or nurse will be able to get it out. Yes, it will be embarrassing, but don't worry — everyone who works in these places has seen a thousand butts and vaginas, and they're wonderfully unshockable. You can ask for a female practitioner if you prefer. (For more on stuck tampons, see "Is Something Wrong?" page 126.)

FACT

The worst thing that could possibly happen . . . has already happened to someone before . . . and they survived it. And you will too!

PERIOD *Challenges*

At School

To be honest, you are very likely to get your period at least some of the time at school. The good news is that *you can manage it*! It's not impossible. The bad news is that managing your period at school can take some energy.

You have to:

 Think ahead and plan for your period. Keep your period pack in your schoolbag at all times! See page 20 for what should go in it.

 Anticipate your period days. If you know it's coming (and let's face it, it's coming sooner or later), be prepared with extra pads or tampons. See page 58 for more info on tracking your cycle.

Check in on your pad or tampon when you've got your period. Check it at break times and lunch *before* you hang out with your friends. That way, you won't worry about whether you're leaking — trust us, it's worth it!

Whether you let your friends know or keep your period to yourself, here's what else you need to know to handle it like a boss.

If you feel comfortable, consider telling your friends that you have your period. I used to be really secretive about it, but then I realized that chances are at least one person is going through the same thing. You can be chocolate-and-bathroom buddies! *Yumi*

Bring your supplies

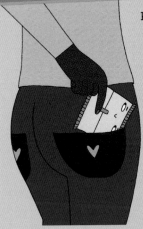

Pack a couple more pads or tampons than you think you'll need, just in case. If your schoolbag has a side pocket, you can put them in there, or just keep your period pack topped up every day.

If you have pockets, you can put two or three pads/tampons in your pocket in the morning before you leave the house and know that you're set for the whole day. If you have a locker, why not leave a whole package in there for when you need it?

Change your pad or tampon at break and lunchtime, before gym, and, if it's a long trip home, after school as well.

You'll want me later!

On school days I make sure I pack all my pads in the morning. I need at least three big pads per day and a tampon. And some chocolate. *Lisa, 15*

Know your restrooms

Figure out which restroom stalls at your school have trash cans or sanitary receptacles, and get in the habit of using those particular stalls once in

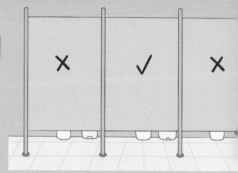

a while, even before you get your period.

If you're in a younger grade, you might discover that the bathrooms don't have sanitary bins in the stalls — which is annoying. There is always a trash can in the actual bathroom itself, but there are often none in the stalls, meaning you have to wrap up your used pad or tampon in toilet paper, take it out of the stall, and place it in the communal trash can.

This is not a big deal, but it's also not great. You deserve a bin that you can use in the privacy of the restroom stall. I recommend you ask your most kick-ass parent (or friend's parent) to speak to the school and ask that bins or receptacles be added in at least one of the stalls. Or, if you're comfortable, go direct — figure out which teacher has the power to create change in your school and explain the situation.

Assert yourself if you need to check in during class

Sometimes you need to change a pad or tampon during class time, although naturally your teachers would prefer you took care of it during lunch and breaks! Still, it's OK if you need to go — just politely ask permission to go to the restroom. If they say no, it's perfectly fine to go up to them and say, "I have my period and I'm going to bleed all over the place if you don't let me go to the bathroom."

Pain at school

Feeling gross? It's all right to take a small amount of acetaminophen or ibuprofen to help you get through. (There's more info on pain management on page 96.) You can also pack foods that make you feel good on these days — ginger helps with bloating and nausea, and celery might make you feel bouncy instead of sluggish. And a bit of dark chocolate can always brighten your period days.

If you feel really unwell, you can go to the nurse's office for a quick rest. But try to avoid calling it a day and going (or staying) home, unless the pain or the bleeding is unmanageable. Missing class puts you at a disadvantage, as you need *all* your learning to become your most awesome self.

Challenges

Playing Sports

You can totally handle being active while you have your period. If you change into a uniform to play sports, this is a good opportunity to swap in a fresh pad or tampon to see you through the game or class. Tampons are a good option if you are running around a lot, since they're invisible — and you won't feel them at all.

Choose athletic shorts that make you feel the most supported — dark colors are good, and a snug fit that makes you feel all tucked in is also good. Some people like to wear bike shorts or leggings underneath their gym shorts, or an extra pair of undies to keep everything secure.

Did you know that exercise can help you feel good when you've got your period? It's actually a recommended way to manage period pain! Exercise releases natural endorphins, which are chemicals that make us feel good. It's a super-helpful tool on your PMS days for this reason too.

Just remember that running around will make you sweaty, and it's common to mistake the feeling of being sweaty down below for the feeling of blood leaking out. If you've just changed your pad, this is very unlikely! But if you want to check, you can always go to the restroom halfway through.

Depending on your relationship with your gym teacher, you might even be able to tell them at the start of class, "I just got my period and would really like to be able to go to the restroom halfway through, if that's OK." Teachers, let me tell you, *love* this kind of communication. It makes them feel respected and it totally stimulates their kindness glands.

If your period is making you feel really unwell or sore, you can also let your teacher know that you need to sit out your game or class.

Some people say that having your period is like a big red button. You just press it and teachers let you skip gym!

But it's because of this goodwill that we think it's important not to abuse it—only skip gym if you really feel like you can't handle it.

PERIOD
Challenges

Swimming

If you can wear a tampon or a menstrual cup, you can go swimming without having to worry about blood. Just change your tampon before you get into the pool (or when you change into your bathing suit) and you'll be fine. See page 46 for info on how to use a tampon or page 54 for how to use a menstrual cup. Ordinary sanitary pads are no good for swimming, since they will absorb water instead of blood. Water can also stop the adhesive glue on pads from working.

If tampons aren't an option for you right now, period bathing suits (which hold special pads in place while you swim) are a thing, just like period panties. They aren't super common, though, and need to be ordered online.

At camp, I had no idea about periods, so I just put a pad in my suit and went for a swim! I thought you could do that! Lucky nobody noticed because I imagine that would've stuck — you know, I would've been the Period Bathing Suit Kid. I remember thinking, "This doesn't actually feel right." It got all waterlogged and heavy — actually, it felt like one of those massive turds in your undies! *Not good at all. Gracie, 37*

For when you really can't swim

If you're not ready for tampons yet, that's OK. No one should ever pressure you or force you to use them. We have heard of a few instances of teachers insisting you should use a tampon so you can take swimming lessons, and frankly, that's not right. Involve a caregiver or parent if you need backup.

If you take swim classes or are on a swim team and you're worried about pushback from teachers or coaches, the first step is to ask your parent or caregiver to write a note for you to explain the situation. Here's a template:

> Dear Teacher,
>
> Please excuse *First Name Last Name* from school swimming today and tomorrow. She has her period and would prefer to sit it out.
>
> Thank you for your understanding.
>
> Sincerely,
> *Parent Name*

However, not everyone has this option.

My mom and dad had jobs that meant they worked like crazy, so getting either one of them to write a note for school was a big deal. I mostly avoided it and managed a lot of my own school stuff. *Yumi*

If, like Yumi, you have parents who aren't that involved in the day-to-day management of your life, you may have to manage the situation yourself. Here are some ways to explain why you can't swim. Some are true and some are a bit bendy with the truth. We always think it's better to be honest, but you'll know better than anyone what will work for your situation.

Swimming days I can usually survive with a tampon and one really thin pad that I wear into the pool. Before I knew how to use tampons, I just wouldn't swim.
Anouk, 15

I can't swim today because I have my period.

I can't swim today because I don't want to.

My mom says I can't swim because I've had a cold for the past week.

My doctor says I shouldn't swim for another week because I'm still a bit flu-y.

Please don't make me swim today because I absolutely do not want to have to explain to you that I have my period.

I want to swim but I can't because I've had a stomach bug.

Our advice to you is always approach the teacher or coach respectfully *and* early. So if swimming or gym is in the afternoon, have a talk with them in the morning so that they know what's coming. Teachers love a bit of warning and appreciate you showing that you're not ignoring gym, or that you haven't forgotten your gym clothes, or that you aren't just being lazy.

This is another good reason to only pull the "period card" when you need to. If you do it all the time, it may not work when you *really* need it!

I can't skip!

If your school or team has super-strict rules about missing gym or swimming and insists on a note from a doctor, then you could:

 Get a note from your doctor that will cover you, about once a month, for the whole year.

 Get your parent or caregiver on board to question rules about needing a doctor to confirm you have periods . . . um, duh . . .

 BRING IT ON: Talk with friends, other students, your favorite teacher, and/or the principal about getting the school rules changed, since menstruation should not be something that students need to get a doctor's note for. It's a natural part of life, not an illness!

PERIOD *Challenges*

Sleepovers

If you don't feel up to going to a sleepover when you've got your period, you don't have to go. But, really, there's no reason to miss out on overnight fun with your friends!

The easiest way to handle having your period during a sleepover is to tell your friend(s). It's not a big deal, and people get their periods all the time. This way, when you take your period pack to the bathroom, it doesn't need to feel like a secret.

Remember that when you change your pad or tampon at a friend's house, it's a good idea to wrap up the used one in toilet paper and put it in the trash can (not the toilet) — just like you'd do at home. If there's no trash can in their bathroom, just wrap it up and put it in the nearest one.

If you don't want to tell anyone at the sleepover that you have your period, you totally don't have to. You'll just need to be organized with your supply of pads, as finding the toilet at night and managing sanitary supplies in a strange house may be tricky!

YOU MIGHT WANT TO PUT YOUR PERIOD PACK SOMEWHERE EASY TO FIND IN THE DARK, OR STASH A COUPLE OF PADS INSIDE THE BATHROOM BEFORE IT'S TIME TO GO TO SLEEP.

Springing a leak at a sleepover

Even though it seems a bit "worst-case scenario," it's totally common for people to leak onto the bedsheets or sleeping bag when they're staying at a friend's house. It's not the end of the world and nobody is going to hate you for doing this.

EEK!

Don't even worry about it! 😊

If it happens, tell your friend what has happened, or tell your friend's parent. Most people are pretty understanding. They will just change and wash the sheets, and life will go on.

Reinforcements

If your flow is heavy or you're worried about spillage, here are some extra precautions you can take:

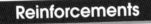 **"Overnight" pads** are extra absorbent and can take a lot of liquid before they start to spill over. Swap out your regular pad for an overnight one right before bedtime.

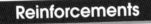 **A tampon as well as a pad** is a pretty good way to keep a regular flow under control. (If the tampon leaks, it'll leak into the pad — pretty clever, huh?) Put the tampon in last thing at night and you might find it lasts right through until morning. But don't keep it in more than eight hours.

I used to have a lot of accidents at night. They didn't really have overnight pads then and you'd wake up in the night thinking everything was all right, but then it'd be a bloodbath because you'd leaked out the back of your pad! To fix this, I would layer a whole bunch of toilet paper and renovate the pad, adding a whole toilet paper extension to the butt-crack area. *Audrey, 37*

 If you're not using tampons, **try wearing a pad with another pair of undies over the top** to keep it firmly in place. You could even wear period panties over your regular pad to add an extra layer of protection.

Thick, dark sweatpants worn as pajamas, or just some decent dark pajamas, will add another layer of protection.

Finally, it is perfectly OK and common to **sleep with a towel under your hips**. Bring one from home if you want to be super prepared.

One time I had a sleepover at a male friend's house and I got my period. The boys were swimming in the backyard pool the whole time and I couldn't tell them the truth, so they kept saying, "Get in, Anouk! Get in!" All night I was worried that I would leak while I was asleep! It was hellish. I ended up using toilet paper for pads overnight and it was actually fine. Hellish, but fine. *Anouk, 15*

Camping

You don't have to miss out on camping just because you've got your period!

Just as campers have to organize food, water, and clothes, you'll need to plan ahead with your supplies. And even if you don't expect to get your period on your next hike or camping adventure, it's worth packing some supplies anyway. Getting surprised is annoying.

There are a few factors that arise while camping that you don't even have to *think* about in the modern world:

 It will probably be harder to get to running water to wash your hands and shower when you're camping.

② If you forget some key supplies, it'll be much harder to run to the store to stock up.

3 You're not usually doing laundry when you're camping, so you need to make sure you've got more than enough clean clothes and underwear to stay feeling fresh, or to manage if there's a spill.

4 Disposing of trash might be something you only get to do at the end of the trip, meaning you'll have to keep it all stored in a bag somewhere—like in your tent or backpack.

It's a good idea to put together a special camping period pack, which is much like a regular period pack with a few additions. It should contain:

⭐ **Enough pads and tampons** for each day of your period. So if you usually bleed for four days and use five pads a day, you will need 20 pads. Plus a few spares.

⭐ **Extra undies and bathing suits** in case of leakage (and also because sometimes it's just nice to have a fresh pair to change into).

⭐ **Hand sanitizer and/or baby wipes.** You don't need to be germ-phobic to want clean hands! It is *great* to have the option to clean your hands when there's no water and soap available, especially before putting in or taking out a tampon or after going to the restroom. Hand sanitizer comes in small travel-size bottles.

⭐ **Three large plastic bags.** Sealable baggies are great, because nothing inside is going to spill out, including smells. The first bag is for all your trash to go into (which you could label clearly as TRASH if you *love* being super organized like Yumi does). The second bag is for dirty undies (which Yumi would gleefully label DIRTY UNDIES). And the third bag is a spare, in case you have the opportunity to throw out the trash bag halfway through your trip and can start a new one.

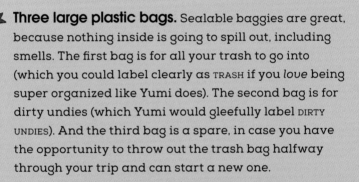

⭐ **One entire set of fresh clothes.** Pack things that aren't your favorites into a separate bag so you won't miss them while they're stashed away. That way, if you leak onto your clothes, or are even just feeling crusty and gross, you've got a glorious clean set of clothes! It's like a little present from your past self!

PERIOD
Challenges

I Live With My Dad

Parent Management

Here's the thing: for most kids, there's an element of having to manage your parents or caregivers, whether it's a mom, a dad, a foster parent, grandparent, or someone else. The people who care for you can't know all your preferences or everything you need. So you have to keep communicating what works and doesn't work, what you like and don't like, and what's going on in your life so that your caregiver can help.

Some caregivers are better at listening to this kind of communication than others! And some might not even need to be told. For instance, some parents might automatically know to stock up on period stuff without having to be asked. Others will need to be asked and then maybe reminded several times.

Dads are no different. Some will be super thoughtful, think of your needs, plan ahead, and be awesome, and some will forget and just need a little more "parent management." The main difference is that most dads haven't had their periods their whole lives like most moms have. Keep that in mind if you live with your dad.

SOME WAYS TO MANAGE DAD
(OR THE PERSON WHO IS HELPING YOU)

1. **Arrange a monthly allowance** where your dad gives you, say, $10–$15 that is just for you to buy period supplies.

2. **Have a dedicated spot** where period supplies live. Teach your dad to notice when they're running low, and to stock up next time he's at the store.

3. **Text your dad** when you need him to get you some pads or tampons. If possible, include a photo of your preferred brand so he gets the right ones.

4. **There are these awesome online "period subscription" services,** where your supplies arrive in the mail every month, like magic! Get your dad's support in finding an online period subscription where you receive your preferred supplies in the mail. The money comes off his credit card and the boxes go to you.

5. **Give him a copy of this book** for his next birthday, Father's Day, or as a random present. Or lend him yours. Point out this page and ask him which way he wants to be "managed." Also encourage him to read the whole book. (Hi, Dad! *waves*) He will learn a lot about periods, and that's a good thing.

Empty the bathroom trash yourself. This isn't much fun, but neither is an overflowing trash can.

 Keep supplies of ibuprofen and acetaminophen around the house, in the car, and in your schoolbag.

⭐ **Change your own sheets** and get the washed ones dried and put away (or even do the laundry yourself). This is a bit boring, but it's worth it for the delightful clean-sheets feeling.

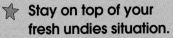

⭐ **Stay on top of your fresh undies situation.** Do your laundry, and pipe up when you need to buy more underwear!

PERIOD

Challenges

Emergency Measures

Everyone has been surprised by their period when they have no stuff — no period pack, no regular supplies in the bathroom cupboard, no emergency stash. Nothing. This happens to everyone — *everyone* — so chances are it'll happen to you. If there's one thing that getting your period teaches you, it's the lifelong skill of resourcefulness. You can:

⭐ **Ask your friends** or other people in the restroom whether they have any spare supplies you could have. You'd be surprised at how often this works! For instance, you could say, "Excuse me, do you happen to have a spare pad or tampon?"

⭐ **Check at the front desk** — many workplaces have a first-aid kit that contains pads. This includes schools, hospitals, and gyms, and they are usually pretty happy to hand them over.

★ Use a little sibling's **diaper**. If you're desperate!

★ Fold up some **toilet paper** and use it to line your undies. It will work for a short amount of time, and luckily, toilet paper tends to be in generous supply in most bathrooms. If you're stuck for a few hours, you might need to check in on it every hour or so.

Our school is pretty cool. Any time you want, you can go to Student Reception and you just have to say "That time of the month" and they'll give you some pads. *Lisa, 15*

★ Use **spare socks** . . . but wet wool can be itchy!

★ Use a mini-pack of **travel tissues**. The perfect shape!

★ Use a small **washcloth or hand towel**, which you can wash when you get home.

To help out your future self, you can also make sure you have emergency supplies stashed in a pocket of every bag you own, the glove box of the family car, and your musical instrument case, just in case. Even just one pad or tampon could save you down the road.

I once went into a pharmacy without any money and asked if I could have some pads and pay them back later. They said yes. I remembered to pay them back, OF COURSE, because WHO COULD FORGET?! *Yumi*

WHAT TO DO IF YOU FEEL LOUSY

There are lots of reasons to feel special about getting your period: you're growing up, your body is changing, and nature is cool. But sometimes you might feel a bit lousy — teary, grumpy, shouty, quiet — and that's normal!

Why am I so grumpy? Is PMS even real?

Yes, it is definitely real.

PMS stands for **premenstrual syndrome**. It's a collection of symptoms that happen during a very specific time in the menstrual cycle — between ovulation and when your period arrives. PMS symptoms stop once bleeding starts. (To get a clear picture of where PMS lands in the cycle, see page 58, but basically it's a few days before you bleed.)

The main symptoms of PMS include:

* irritability
* mood swings
* anxiety
* depression
* swelling
* bloating
* breast tenderness
* headaches

It doesn't affect everyone, but it can be a problem for up to 30 percent of teens, who can experience some or all of the symptoms. Those with period pain are more likely to also have PMS.

Despite so many teenagers and adult women having PMS, the cause is still not fully understood — although it is related to period hormone patterns in some way. You'd be surprised to know how many grown women, who've been bleeding for years, honestly believe they're just cranky and don't realize they've been experiencing PMS until the PMS is over. Every month!

There are effective ways to treat PMS symptoms:

The Pill

Because PMS is related to fluctuating menstrual cycle hormones, actually using some hormones can help with symptoms. The most useful of these can be found in contraceptive pills, which can be used in the "usual" way — in other words, taking them every day — or by taking them just during the second phase of the menstrual cycle. It's best to talk to a doctor to figure out what your specific needs are.

Antidepressants

Low doses of some antidepressant medications also work for some people, since mood changes seem to result from the interaction between menstrual hormones and brain chemicals.

Counseling

Similarly, a certain type of counseling technique used for treating depression — called cognitive behavioral therapy — can work. Talk to your doctor to learn more.

Over-the-counter supplements

Calcium supplements can be effective for some PMS symptoms. Some people find that chasteberry extract or magnesium helps, and vitamin B6 and evening primrose oil have been used as well.

Before my period, I feel like crying

You know what? It's totally OK to just feel your feelings.

Remember that the emotions will pass — especially once you start to bleed. It can make you feel better to have a cry — call a friend, sit with a parent, or have some "you" time with an emotional movie or a favorite book. Plenty of brave, fierce, and awesome people have needed to snuggle up with a hot-water bottle and chocolate and just spend some time feeling like crap in order to feel better.

Personally, I like to do a boxing class and just punch it out. *Yumi*

Eating well can help PMS too

PMS can cause a feeling of bloating and cravings for junk food! But trust us: excessive sugar (like candy), salt (like chips), and caffeine (like sodas) are really *no help*, before your period or when you're bleeding and already feeling a bit gross.

Instead, aim to eat lots of nutritious foods that make you feel zingy and vibey, like fruit, fish, and vegetables. They're good for you all the time, but especially before or when you're bleeding. At the very least, they won't make you feel worse. And then if you need to eat some chocolate to cheer yourself up, it will be balanced out by all the nutritious food already in your body. Smaller meals and regular exercise can also help PMS.

My period usually drains out most of my energy. The great thing about my first period was I stayed home with Mom. We went out for breakfast, which was really nice. I told my friends I had gotten my period and they were like, "Oh my gosh, do you know how awful this is? Do you have a headache? Do you have stomach pain?" And I was like, "It's not that bad!" except the next day I was like, "You were right, it is that bad!" *Tans, 13*

HOW TO HANDLE PERIOD PAIN

Most people don't get any period pain for six to twelve months after their first period, but then it becomes fairly common. Very common, actually – 75 percent or more of teenagers will experience mild or moderate period pain, and 10 percent or so may get severe pain.

Before you worry too much, though, here are some fast facts:

 Most period pain lasts for only one or two days.

 Period pain treatments are very effective in most cases.

 If the simple treatments don't work, there are other options.

I know this sounds grim, but most of us with mild period pain get used to it . . . and it becomes just a bit of background noise. *Yumi*

What causes the period pain?

As the lining of the uterus begins to shed at the beginning of your period, the cells in this lining release a hormone called prostaglandin. This prostaglandin helps the muscular wall of the uterus contract, which squeezes out the lining more effectively. Sometimes there's a bit of overkill — too much prostaglandin, too much muscle contraction — and it goes into a kind of cramp.

In people with bad period pain, levels of prostaglandin can generally be higher. The prostaglandin from the uterus can also cause other physical effects like nausea, vomiting, bloating, and headaches.

Prostaglandin also causes your intestines to wake up and get active — so it's common to poop more at the beginning of your period!

I was really young — just 10 years old — and nobody else in my school had it. I remember just feeling really sick at school and having really, really bad pain. When I got home, I realized that I had it. The next day all the other kids were like, "Are you OK?" And I was like, "Yeah, I got my period." Because I was the first person BY FAR to get my period, everyone was super interested! I think a lot of friends thought it would actually hurt having the blood coming out, so I was able to explain that it was just the feeling sick leading up to your period, and that the pain was kind of in your body (not in your vagina). *Nadine, 35*

Some people find just one of these treatments works, while others use a combination. Experiment and find out what works for you!

Period pain relievers

Ibuprofen

Ibuprofen is the most effective medication for period pain that you can buy at the supermarket or over the counter at a pharmacy (you don't need a prescription). Ibuprofen can have lots of different brand names, so look for the word "ibuprofen" in the fine print — that is the actual name of the active ingredient, which is a kind of nonsteroidal anti-inflammatory drug (NSAID). It works best if taken as soon as your period starts, before the pain hits. That's because it counteracts the release of the prostaglandin hormones in the uterus that cause cramping and other symptoms such as nausea, bloating, and headaches. Taking ibuprofen according to the instructions on the bottle can help with all these symptoms. And if one brand doesn't work, try a different one next time (though not on the same day!).

Remember to always stick to the recommended dosage for painkillers, and check with your parent or caregiver before you take anything!

Acetaminophen

Acetaminophen is a commonly used painkiller, often taken for headaches. It's effective for period pain, though not usually as effective as ibuprofen.

These tablets can have side effects, as with any medication. But in general the benefit of period pain relief outweighs the side effects.

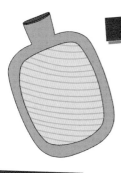

Heat

Lying down with a heating pad or hot-water bottle over your lower tummy or lower back can help. Combining this with your favorite movie and some occasional loud complaining can enhance the soothing effect . . . although this has not been scientifically proven!

Exercise

It sounds weird, but exercise really helps period pain! Sometimes going for a run or doing something very physically active — like a fitness class, biking, or even skipping rope — really helps. It can get your circulation going and make you feel happier, plus distract you from the discomfort.

Relaxation

When we say "relaxation," we're talking about relaxation techniques such as breathing exercises, yoga, meditation, and visualizations. But lying on the couch and eating comfort food can be OK, too.

These techniques can take some practice, but are great for managing pain in the rest of your life too.

Complementary medicine and supplements

Vitamin B1 and fish oil supplements

These don't necessarily work as a treatment WHEN you get your period. But some research is showing that taking 100 milligrams of vitamin B1 a day can reduce period pain over time. It's possible that fish oil supplements can help in this way too. Fish oil supplements contain omega-3 fatty acids, which you also get from food. Oily fish are the best sources of omega-3 fatty acids, and plant-based sources include flaxseed, soybeans, walnuts, and wild rice.

Other vitamins and supplements

Magnesium supplements seem to be beneficial for period pain. Some studies have looked at calcium, zinc, vitamin E, vitamin D, and ginger powder and found that they might help.

Traditional Chinese medicine and acupuncture

Herbs used in traditional Chinese medicine — like ginger, licorice root, and cinnamon bark — can help period pain, as can acupuncture.

CAN I MAKE MY PERIODS STOP?

If you don't want your period at all, you can suppress it instead of managing it.

There might be a medical or health-related reason for stopping periods. Or you might decide after a few months or years of having monthly bleeds that you'd like to reduce their frequency or intensity.

People with very heavy or painful periods or bad PMS (see page 92) can benefit from medical treatments that make periods lighter or less painful. This might also mean less time off school, not having to skip sports, and not having to miss fun. (See "Is Something Wrong?" on page 126). Another scenario is periods causing distress because of gender identity (see page 106).

For some people, there isn't a specific health reason for stopping periods. Some might want to stop them short-term because of travel, a school formal, or some other convenience-related issue. Others are happy to take a break from periods for months, or even years.

When I first started getting my period, this would have been the first chapter I'd have turned to. *Yumi*

MYTH BUSTER

Some people worry that it's not safe to stop yourself from bleeding regularly. Back in the days before there was any really effective contraception, many women spent a lot of their lives without periods, whether from pregnancy or breastfeeding. Many women would go for years without a period. It wasn't harmful to skip your period then, and it isn't harmful to do it now, either.

Today, people can choose to stop or reduce the frequency of periods by using medications or treatments that need a doctor's prescription. While it's important to discuss any prescription medication with your doctor to make sure it's safe for you, the actual lack of bleeding is generally safe.

The Pill

The simplest way to suppress menstruation is to take hormonal contraception. The one that's been around the longest is "the Pill." Getting the Pill involves a visit to the doctor, a checkup, and, if all is well, a prescription. This is a tried-and-tested, safe, and very effective treatment for period pain. The Pill was designed as a contraceptive (in other words, to prevent pregnancy), but many people take it just for period pain.

The way it works is that it contains hormones that mimic some of the natural period hormones.

THE PILL

The Pill hormones "talk" to the ovaries (telling them not to ovulate) and to the uterus (telling it not to prepare a thick lining this month).

A cycle of the Pill usually involves taking 28 daily tablets — 21 hormone pills, plus seven sugar pills that don't actually do anything. Taking the sugar pills means your body has a break from the Pill hormones. For most people, this sugar-pill week causes your body to have a hormone-withdrawal bleed, which is similar to a regular menstrual bleed, but lighter and less painful. It's lighter and less painful because the Pill hormones have slowed down the usual buildup of uterine lining.

If you keep taking the hormone pills instead of the sugar pills over those seven days, you stop your body from having the hormone-withdrawal bleed.

Meaning, simply: you don't have a bleed.

Many people on the Pill choose to take the hormone pills continuously — maybe for three months, maybe for a year. It's not a total guarantee that you won't bleed at all during this time — something called "breakthrough bleeding" can happen, which means you have a light period-like bleed while taking the hormone pills.

These effects on your period cycle are temporary — they only last as long as you take the Pill. When you stop, your cycle returns to its natural state.

I once made it to the state finals for diving (!) and I didn't know how to use a tampon. I didn't want to miss out, so I got a prescription for the Pill from my doctor. *Yumi*

Other hormonal contraceptive methods

As well as the Pill, there are more involved hormonal methods that can stop you from getting your period. One is a contraceptive implant that is inserted into your arm by a doctor.

Another is the hormone IUD (intrauterine device). Getting it involves a simple procedure where you take off your undies, lie down on an exam table, and have a doctor find their way up inside your vagina using an instrument called a speculum. The doctor then puts a small, T-shaped device inside the uterus, which releases the hormone slowly over three to seven years (depending on the device). It's a really good treatment for heavy menstrual bleeding.

hormone reservoir

flexible arms

Taking any of these hormone contraceptive methods is not a guarantee that periods will skip or stop. You should talk to your doctor first about whether any of these options would work for you, and what the risks and side effects are. Some people will still experience irregular or ongoing bleeding while using these methods. IUD insertion can be painful. Some people also react poorly to any hormonal birth control.

It might be worth having a chat with family members to see what has worked for them, whether there were any side effects for them, and whether they experienced anything negative from using these methods.

Society expects things of my body that aren't right for me

Some people find that the body they are born with makes other people expect them to be a "girl" or a "boy," when this is not how *they* identify. Those who are assigned female at birth (AFAB) might grow up identifying as boys (or vice versa); they might identify as both or neither; or they might be unsure. They might have done lots of things since childhood to affirm their identities and help people see them as their true gender, such as the way they dressed, the name or nickname they used, and other choices they've made that feel good for themselves. The umbrella term for this is "transgender," or just "trans."

As puberty approaches, the idea of getting a period can be *beyond* scary — it can be the worst thing imaginable. But it totally depends on the person — even if they don't feel fully like a girl, the idea of a period might be OK, or the trans identity may be something that comes later.

Transgender children, adolescents, and adults have existed for as long as time. Just as we now have the medical technology to help girls and women manage their periods, doctors can also help transgender adolescents who don't want to have any periods. Doctors can prescribe hormones to try to block or stop periods and other physical changes.

Fortunately, society is gaining understanding of transgender people and their rights and needs. If this feels familiar to you, the best option is to speak to a parent or caregiver, as well as your doctor or an adult you trust.

There are some good websites with information as well—your doctor can direct you to the most relevant ones.

I was pretty fortunate because my periods stopped a month or so after I started taking testosterone. I was presenting as male for a long while before I started taking it. Because of my dysphoria, my own brain made it feel disastrous to have to go and buy tampons. But now, not so much. I have a beard, and I rarely get misgendered. Recently my testosterone dipped and I got a bleed, and I just went to a drugstore and bought tampons. I said to the shop assistant, "Where are your sanitary items?" and she said, "You mean, female hygiene products?" and I said, "No. I mean sanitary items." *Nevo, 22*

HYGIENE AND YOUR PERIOD

There is no law dictating what should and shouldn't happen during your period, and that includes showering and managing your hygiene. If you want to go your own way with this, that's totally OK. Different people have different preferences, but this is how some people like to keep clean when they have their period

Take a shower every day

If you've been a bit slack about daily showers before puberty, now that you're getting your period, it's a good time to start being more disciplined. Your skin and hair tends to get oily more quickly now, so it might be worth the extra showering.

Showering is the perfect time to refresh. Take out your tampon, throw away your pad, hop in the shower, and give your vulva and vagina a good rinse with water or plain soap.

Once you finish your shower, dry off and put in a new pad or tampon and fresh underwear. Period blood is not dirty or gross, but it does have a color, and if it sticks around long enough, it can give off a smell — kind of a rusty odor. Showering regularly is a good way to make sure you feel fresh and clean. You might also like to use dark-colored towels to hide any little period stains that might appear when you dry between your legs. If you don't have access to a shower, a washcloth soaked in warm water and mild soap works for cleaning your armpits and vulva.

SOAP AND YOUR VULVA

Water or water with some unscented soap is the best thing to use for your vulva around your anus and perineum—in other words, all the outside parts. You do *not* need to get soap up inside the vagina. Avoid wipes, gels, deodorants, and douches, as these can irritate the skin and kill the helpful bacteria that live inside your vagina.

Wash your hands!

When using the bathroom, you should be washing your hands with soap. Take extra care to remember to do this on days when you've got your period. The best practice is to wash your hands before you change your pad or tampon. Then wash your hands again thoroughly afterward.

There have been lots of people in my life who have good showering hygiene, but then would hop out of their towel and put on the same clothes they were wearing before. If you're going to do that, try to keep your clothes clean, and mind the smells that can come from armpits and unwashed bras as well. *Yumi*

WHAT DO BOYS THINK OF PERIODS?

Who cares? **Just joking.**
(SORT OF.)

What boys think about periods doesn't have anything to do with you — so it really doesn't matter what they think. But if your friends are boys, of course it matters. Your brother, your boyfriend, your teammates, your dad — you might want them to understand this important part of your life.

If you're pretty new to periods, chances are the boys in your life will still be learning too. Many boys end up being pretty cool and supportive and respectful around periods, but it can take a few tries before they get there. They don't have this book or your period knowledge, and cis boys will never have to actually go through it the way you will, so it can be an adjustment.

Just like you care what your friends or brothers are going through in their lives, it matters that they care about what you're going through in yours. So talk to them about it in a matter-of-fact way. Answer their questions if you feel like it, or else you could lend them this book. The "Being an Ally" section on page 112 is a good place for them to start.

But remember, you're the one who's most affected by your period — not them. So make sure they follow your lead.

And unless they plan on moving to a world without women, all the boys you know now will — for the rest of their lives — have to deal with people who'll have periods. Understanding periods can only be a good thing for them, right now and into the future.

When little brothers or male classmates act all spun-out and horrified by periods, it's pretty annoying. We're not a horror show just because we bleed. I think it's at this time in our development it really hits home that some people don't mature as quickly as others. *Yumi*

I got my period in sixth grade. Me and my friends have a code word for periods so we can help each other out and lend each other pads and stuff. Our code word is "Guys, guys, guys, guys!" But now that we're in junior high school, everyone is really comfortable talking about periods. If guys are talking about gross things like their dicks or porn they've watched, then we interrupt them by shouting "VAGINAL BLEEDING." Sometimes I don't shout, I just give them the rundown on how the uterus works. *Dee Dee, 13*

BEING AN ALLY: A PRIMER

THIS CHAPTER IS FOR YOU IF YOU'RE NOT SOMEONE WHO MENSTRUATES, BUT YOU WANT TO BE A GOOD ALLY TO THOSE WHO DO.

LISTEN

If your friend just wants to vent about their period, be a good listener. That is a huge part of just being a good friend in general.

BE SYMPATHETIC

You might not be able to put yourself in our shoes completely, but try.

DON'T ACT LIKE WE'RE DISGUSTING

We're not. Dog poop is disgusting. Vomit is disgusting. We're just fine, thank you.

DON'T BLAME OUR BAD MOOD ON PERIODS. MAYBE YOU'RE JUST ANNOYING?

"Do you have your period?" is just the worst question, even if the answer is yes. Never, ever ask it!

BUT YOU CAN STILL (SILENTLY) ACKNOWLEDGE THAT A PERIOD MAY BE MAKING EVERYDAY THINGS TOUGHER FOR US THAN THEY ARE FOR YOU

YOU WILL NEVER KNOW.

WHAT CAN YOU DO INSTEAD?

"What can I do to help?" is one of the greatest questions ever asked. Ask it again. And again. Aaaaand again.

STAND UP FOR US

If someone else is giving us a hard time for reasons beyond our control, your support is absolutely vital and deeply appreciated.

LET OTHER NON-BLEEDERS KNOW WHEN THEY'RE BEING INAPPROPRIATE

Yeah, bullying, shaming, and mockery about getting a period actually aren't cool. You may have to call out these behaviors if they're coming from what we call NON-allies (also sometimes known as "jerks"). If you can assist, that's less work for the person who's bleeding to have to do.

FORGIVE YOURSELF!

Maybe you were once the kid going, "Ewww, gross!" and shrieking at the sight of a pad. That's OK if you've changed. No one starts out perfect. We all grow and evolve.

YOU MAY NEED TO DO A SUPPLY RUN

Us: "Can you go to my bag and get a pad?"

You: "Yes, Yes, I can."

PERIODS AND THE ENVIRONMENT

The thing about using ordinary pads and tampons from the supermarket is that they (and all the plastic packaging that comes with them) are disposable . . . which means that when you're done with them, they go into a landfill. They're not environmentally friendly.

Before you start feeling guilty about polluting the environment with your period, *give yourself a break*. Remember that if you're reading this book, chances are you're relatively new to your period or are still waiting for it to start. If reducing waste is something you care about, you can become an expert in managing your period using environmentally sustainable methods when you're absolutely ready.

So, how can you reduce your impact on the environment? Here are ideas to suit different budgets and preferences.

Tampons

Most tampons are made of cotton or synthetic rayon, or a combination of both. As a first step, look for organic, pure cotton tampons, as these are better for the environment than tampons where the ingredients are undisclosed. Bear in mind that even 100 percent organic tampons can take upward of a hundred years to completely break down (although they do break down eventually), and the single-use plastic wrapping they come in can take centuries.

Plastic tampon applicators are also a single-use plastic, so it's more environmentally friendly to use brands with cardboard applicators. (To be clear, there's no actual reason applicators are any better than using your fingers to insert a tampon!) You can also find reusable rubber applicators that you wash and carry.

Pads

A plastic, disposable sanitary pad will take between five hundred and eight hundred years to break down in a landfill, and wrapping used ones in plastic makes it even harder for them to break down. Thousands of tons of disposable sanitary waste are generated every month all over the world!

Don't freak out, though. Look for pads with minimal packaging that don't use bleaching. Recycle their boxes. Once you're comfortable managing your period, you'll probably find you can use smaller pads and fewer of them, or even just liners, to manage the lighter flow days. This will have less impact on the environment.

Period panties

Period panties are great! They're comfortable and reusable, and they last a long time, especially if you wash them using cold water and gentle soap and then hang them up to dry. The only downside is that they're not as effective on the first one to two days of your period, when your flow is heaviest.

Reusable pads

Reusable cloth pads are becoming more popular for environmental reasons because you don't need to throw anything out. Like period undies, you can wash them in cold water and reuse them for years. They're gaining traction for some people with sensitive skin because, unlike regular pads, they don't contain plastic and have fewer skin irritants.

The downside is that cloth pads can be a little bulky for smaller bodies, and they are not usually sold in supermarkets — so look for them in eco-stores and online.

To manage my period, I use cloth pads. They're really soft and absorbent. The nighttime ones are really ridiculously huge so you don't get the butt-crack leak! To go out for a full day, I need to take four cloth pads with me, or three if it's my first day. I like to change my pads often. The pads have little buttons on them, so I usually fold them and click the buttons together and put them back in the bag — used ones roll up neatly like a reusable shopping bag. I have a special bucket, and Mom cleans them and dries them on the clothesline, leaving them out in the sun for one to two days until they're good and dry. You treat them like cloth diapers — wash them in cold water and don't use the dryer (it shortens their life span). They cost between $12 and $30. Lots of little home businesses make them. I like them because they're good for nature, and because we're hippies. *Tans, 13*

Menstrual cups, or "moon cups," are the most cost-effective and environmentally sensitive way to manage your period, as the cups can be reused for up to 10 years. They do not need to be changed as often as pads or tampons, making them handy for travel and other long commitments, and they create zero waste. They are usually leak-proof and do not emit an odor. The downside is they take some practice getting used to!

The main environmental impact of moon cups is in their production and shipping. Their day-to-day use just requires small amounts of water and soap to clean them. For a lot more on menstrual cups, see page 54.

Free bleeding

Have you ever noticed that in TV shows where people are stranded on desert islands, no one ever talks about managing their periods by free bleeding? Which is weird, because presumably that's what all the people who menstruate are doing, unless they happened to wash up on the island with years' worth of pads and tampons and menstrual cups . . .

Free bleeding is the idea of managing your period without any products, just letting the blood flow free. If you're nervous about leakage onto your clothes, this is something to try when you're more familiar with your flow or your cycle is more regular, and you know when your lighter days are likely to be. It's also a good idea to wear darker undies and clothes when you try it.

You can do free bleeding when you're home just chillin', when you know that your flow is really light and will be captured on your underwear (which you can just wash out). You already free bleed in the shower and the blood just washes down the drain, which is awesome.

These days, there are period activists who advocate for free bleeding throughout your whole cycle. They do this for a number of reasons: because they believe that we shouldn't be ashamed of menstruating (which is true — nearly half the population does it regularly!), or because they feel more comfortable bleeding onto their clothes than capturing the blood with a pad, tampon, or cup. Some are also trying to create less waste and landfill by avoiding disposable period products entirely.

ABOUT THE VAGINA

The vagina is important enough to get its own chapter in this book.

A lot of kids aren't aware that they even have a vagina until they are older. (They just know about pee holes and poop holes.) This is totally normal!

But as you get older, you may develop a sense that it's there. Around puberty, it's common to start to have a clear or milky discharge from your vagina. Sexy feelings or thoughts may cause discharge and new sensations in that area too. It's all normal and part of growing up. (For more on discharge, see page 60.)

How can I see my vagina?

Standing in front of a mirror in the nude won't actually help you see it — it's in a spot that's tricky to see straight on.

The best way to see your vagina is to crouch down and hold a hand mirror between your legs. You could also lie on your back with your head propped up on a pillow, and bend your knees up before trying to see it with the mirror.

To see the opening of the vagina, you may need to use your fingers to separate the labia, or folds of skin that usually cover the vaginal opening when your legs are together. Even then, you might not be able to see much.

When the vagina is resting, its walls often touch each

other. You can put your clean finger in gently to separate the walls and try to look farther in.

People often mistakenly refer to all their "parts" as a "vagina," but all of the outside part that fits inside your underpants — including your urethra (pee hole), labia, and clitoris (the highly sensitive nub just above your urethra) — is called the "vulva." The vagina is just the tube between your vulva and your cervix. The cervix is part of the uterus, but it's narrow and has only a small, slit-like opening between your uterus and the rest of the world. (During childbirth, this small opening expands massively under the influence of special hormones.) It's difficult to get beyond the cervix without being a doctor — but when you have your period, blood travels through your cervix from your uterus and into your vagina.

THE VAGINA IS A TUBE OF MUSCLE THAT GROWS BIGGER DURING PUBERTY AND DEVELOPS A SOFT, SPONGY LINING.

AWESOME PUBERTY

Puberty? I'm a big fan!

You won't get your period unless you're going through puberty — it's part of a package deal.

Puberty involves lots of amazing changes inside your body and out. It's nature's way of getting your body ready to be able to reproduce. It can definitely feel as though an alien has taken over. Thanks to a heap of new hormones, puberty makes your body do weird stuff like sprout underarm and pubic hair and change proportions. Puberty can also send you into emotional spinouts. But if you think about it, puberty is also pretty awesome. How cool is it that your body just starts changing you into the adult version of yourself — without an instruction manual!

What a roller coaster!

My son has been a massive *Alice in Wonderland* fan all his life (he even had an *Alice*-themed tea party for his 16th birthday). Some of Alice's adventures remind me of what puberty can feel like — like when her body suddenly grows and shrinks after she takes a bite of cake or has a sip of cordial, and it just feels out of control. *Dr. Melissa*

Help! I just hit puberty

Puberty can feel sudden and unstoppable — even though it's actually been on its way for quite a long time. It's as if you've been floating gently down a river and then you suddenly come to a waterfall! You may not know it, but the changes in your body actually began one to two years before your first period. And *when* that happens it's different for everyone.

Random puberty facts

- ★ All animals—from alligators to bees to humans to salmon to zebra finches—go through some sort of puberty.

- ★ During puberty, you will grow faster than at any other time in your life (except your first two years).

- ★ On average, people get taller by around 25 percent during puberty!

- ★ Your limbs get proportionately longer, and because your body grows, your head gets proportionately smaller.

- ★ The brain grows only a little in size during puberty, but goes through massive changes to its different parts and electrical circuits.

⭐ Changes in the brain's "wiring" in puberty help with things like problem solving, hand-eye coordination, understanding emotions better, and being able to think about and "get" where another person is coming from.

Other stuff that often happens in puberty

These are the obvious ones, because you can see them.

 You'll grow breasts and pubic hair.

⭐ Skin and hair get more oily, which contributes to pimples.

 Armpits grow hair, as well as develop a type of sweat gland that attracts skin bacteria that cause BO (body odor).

⭐ Your body shape changes partly because of your bone "architecture" and the way muscles and fat are arranged. Your weight also increases due to everything growing. (To be fair, you've been growing and changing your whole life, but puberty just speeds things up!)

Everyone's body is different, and puberty is different for everyone. Height and weight, skin and hair color, individual facial features, genitals, body shapes and sizes — there are amazing variations even within families.

During puberty, your brain changes, which has an effect on your thoughts and feelings. You might feel overly emotional — super angry, or sad, or anything in between — for no reason. You might start to feel self-conscious or worry that your body is weird compared with everyone else's. (You also might not, in which case — yay!)

If you do feel self-conscious, try to remember that feeling like you're a freak — or uncoordinated, or hideous — will likely pass, and it's also not true. No matter what is happening to your body, you are fine the way you are. Your brain is just Going Through Some Stuff.

On the plus side, those brain changes also mean that we develop the ability to start seeing things from another person's point of view. So try to remember that everyone around you is going through the same thing, and different things, at different times. It's kind of amazing!

FUN FACT ABOUT PERIODS

The only animals that have periods are humans, apes, monkeys, elephant shrews, bats, and—as recently discovered—the spiny mouse. Other animals have similar hormone cycles, but they absorb their uterine lining internally—it doesn't flow outside the body.

125

IS SOMETHING WRONG?

Periods happen naturally for most of us who are born with ovaries, a uterus, and a vagina. For some, things happen that make us think something's wrong. Many teenage girls worry there's a problem. I always hope to be able to reassure them. Sometimes I think there may be an issue and will recommend getting a checkup from a doctor. But most of the time, medical causes of period problems in teenagers are common and easy enough to manage.

My best friend in high school didn't start puberty until she was almost 14, and her periods didn't start until she was 16. She remained petite while the rest of the girls got taller and grew curves. The thing I remember most is how mean some of the kids at school were. They called her nicknames and snickered quietly so that she could hear but the teachers couldn't. And the worst thing was — this came from other girls. Even though these girls liked her too; she was a really lovely person, popular with the boys, smart, and caring! Being humiliated like this was her private agony for those first three and a half years of high school.

Having a really amazing mom helped her get through some of that pain, and I hope that having good friends (like me!) also helped. But what is it with the need to be mean to people who are on a different timeline than you? Being mean is the opposite of anything even remotely cool. *Dr. Melissa*

My period hasn't come yet

❝ I'm 15 and haven't gotten my period yet. My sister who is two years younger than me has gotten hers. Is there something wrong with me? ❞

When those around you get their period and you don't, it can be kind of awesome at first — the longer you can put off dealing with pads, bleeding, and PMS, the better!

Then months go by, and maybe you start thinking, "Is something wrong with me?"

The easiest way to reassure yourself is to check the rest of your body's changes. Remember: puberty is so much more than periods! See page 122 for more.

✦ How much taller have you grown in the past two years?

★ Have your breasts and pubic hair developed a little or a lot?

✦ Have you noticed more subtle things, like your voice deepening a bit and more facial and body hair? (This happens very noticeably in boys, but girls get this too.)

Periods begin late in puberty, when most of the above changes are well underway. It's usually at least two years after breast development before you can expect your first period.

The timing of puberty (your age when it first starts) is partly controlled by your genes — so if your female relatives were older than average to start, chances are you will be too. From a medical point of view, we recommend a checkup if:

★ Your breasts started growing by age 10 or earlier, but you have not started your periods by the age of 14.

★ Your breasts started growing at age 14, but you have not started your periods by the age of 16.

If either of these scenarios sounds like you, there's still no need to panic. You could be among that small percentage of people whose natural puberty timeline is just a little later.

Reasons for getting your period after everyone else

There are medical and physical conditions that cause a delay or an absence of periods. One of the more common reasons is extreme exercise. Another is insufficient nutrition, which can be due to an eating disorder, or poverty, or living in a country where drought, war, or other causes of food insecurity have led to famine.

Most of the other causes relate to hormonal problems, and it can take a bunch of hormone tests to figure out what's going on. The hormone tests are done by doctors using a blood sample.

(Don't be freaked out by this — it's easy for a nurse to take a blood sample from one of the veins in the crook of the elbow. They're big and close to the surface. There's a small needle sting, but you can handle it.)

Other causes include genetic conditions that result in some part of the menstrual cycle control centers (from the brain to the ovaries) not getting programmed to begin to cycle.

Very rarely, the vagina and uterus are absent from birth. This might go undetected even after puberty, and only comes to light when the absence of periods causes the patient to see a doctor.

Finally, your period can come late because of an earlier medical condition, such as cancer in childhood. Treatments involving chemotherapy or radiation affect the organs that control puberty and periods, and this can affect physical development later on.

How do I talk to a doctor about this?

If you're thinking of going to your doctor to talk about your period starting late, the conversation might go like this:

You: "I'm worried about the fact that I haven't gotten my period yet. I'm XX years old. All my friends have gotten their period."

Then the doctor will ask you questions like these:

How old was your mother when she got her period? What about your older sisters?

OK, can I ask you a few questions about puberty? That will help us figure out when we might expect your periods. When did you notice your breasts growing? What about pubic hair? Have you had a growth spurt? Have you noticed discharge or fluid in your undies? For how long?

Now some questions about your general health. Has your weight changed much in recent months? Have you changed the type or amount of food you eat? What about exercise — what's an average week like? Ever had any chronic or serious illnesses?

Then the doctor might weigh you (though if it is not medically necessary, you can ask not to be weighed), measure your height, show you a diagram of puberty development, and ask you at what stage you think your body is. From there, they should be able to give you some advice or reassurance.

My periods are really irregular

❝ I was wondering, is it normal not to get your period every 28 days? I'm 16 years old and sometimes it's late, like every 30 days, and sometimes it's early, like 26 or 27 days. Is this normal? **❞**

❝ I'm 15 and I first got my period when I was 12. It was on a normal cycle every month, then it started to come between three and six months, and then about six months ago I had weeklong periods for three months, and then it just stopped again. I know cycles take a while to adjust, but this just feels weird. **❞**

Periods really *are* confusing! Sometimes, you wait and wait for that first period, and it finally arrives — yay! You're a master menstruator! Then . . . *nothing happens.*

You might be wondering if (a) it was all a dream, (b) it was a false start and you're being tricked! or (c) something really bad is going on. But chances are, everything's fine — it's really common for your period to be irregular for the first couple of years.

Two years after getting their very first period, most new menstruators will fall into a regular period pattern, called the "menstrual cycle." (See page 148 for how the menstrual cycle works.)

The cycle is counted in days, from the first day of one period to the first day of the next period. The cycle does not have to be EXACTLY the same each time: it can vary from between 22 and 45 days when you're a teenager, to between 22 and 35 days once your body has finished growing.

In the letter from the 16-year-old, the menstrual cycle that varies from 26 to 30 days is considered completely regular.

On the other hand, the 15-year-old who wrote in might be experiencing irregular cycles, since it's been more than two years since her first period and she might be having cycles lasting more than 45 days.

A really helpful way to track your cycle is to use a period tracker app for a few months. It helps guide you and your doctor as to whether any tests need to be done.

If your cycle has been regular but has become irregular after two to three years, or if it has *never* been regular and it's been more than two years since your first period, then it could be time to get a checkup.

A common cause of periods becoming irregular is stress. It's difficult to say how much stress is "too much," because everyone responds to stress differently. But being significantly stressed over time — due to school, family, or friend issues — can be enough to influence the pattern of your periods. Changes to your eating patterns or weight can also change the regularity of your cycle.

In teenagers, truly irregular periods are often caused by hormone imbalances or problems. The most common of these is a condition called polycystic ovary syndrome, or PCOS (see page 140).

QUESTIONS FOR DR. MELISSA

My periods have stopped. Am I pregnant?

❝ I'm really worried about my period. I've missed a full month and it's going on to the second month now and I'm scared something's wrong with me. I've never had sex but can I be pregnant? ❞

If you've never had sex, then no, you can't be pregnant.

It's totally normal for your mind to "go there" when you miss a period, because we're often taught that missed periods = pregnancy. But there are lots of reasons why you can miss a period that have nothing to do with pregnancy.

It might help you to remember that there are only a few ways pregnancy can happen:

★ The most common way is from sexual intercourse. During unprotected penis-in-vagina sex, fluid called "semen" is squirted out from the penis into the vagina. This is called ejaculation.

Semen contains sperm. If sperm fertilizes an egg, that can result in pregnancy (see page 146).

★ Sometimes a guy pulls out his penis before he ejaculates and squirts his semen outside the vagina. Fluid containing sperm can still have leaked inside the vagina before the final squirt, where it can travel up the vagina to fertilize an egg.

If there has not been unprotected sex where a penis ejaculated inside the vagina, but you have been intimate with someone, you could become pregnant the following ways:

★ Your partner's wearing a condom, but it breaks or slips off during intercourse due to improper use. Therefore the sex was unprotected, so semen could be present and may fertilize an egg.

★ Sometimes there's semen close to the opening of the vagina, even if the penis didn't go all the way inside it. Sperm are good swimmers and, in the right conditions, they can travel up toward the uterus and, *very rarely*, fertilize an egg. This is a low-risk situation, and the semen would have to physically touch the opening of the vagina where it's moist — it won't swim on your outside skin.

In these scenarios, pregnancy is possible. Not *likely*, just possible.

If NONE of these scenarios have happened and a sperm has never been near your body, let alone *inside* of your body, then pregnancy is not possible.

Period poverty

Period poverty is the condition of not being able to afford menstrual products. Maybe it affects you and your loved ones. Period poverty happens when other needs —for example, the need for food or shelter — come before spending money on menstrual products. Being in that situation has big implications. For some girls, period poverty might mean they cannot attend school when they have their period.

More and more, people are recognizing that period poverty is an important cause of inequality. There is a global push to make menstrual products free. Some countries are removing the "Tampon Tax," to ensure that tampons and other menstrual products are classified as "essential items" by the government, rather than "luxury items" that do get taxed. Lots of young people have been involved in the protesting of this tax.

Another reason that some people don't have access to menstrual products is the stigma associated with periods. Stigma is a negative attitude or feeling (such as shame or disgrace) cast over people for something they are or something they have done. Stigma can be so powerful that it can leave people feeling isolated or depressed. Sadly, there are still a lot of beliefs about periods that make it impossible for people who are menstruating to be part of a community. But no one should ever be shamed for having periods!

My periods are super heavy

❝ Hey . . . this might seem a bit gross, but my periods are really heavy . . . and there are these huge blobs throughout it! Is this normal? I've only had my period for six months. ● Is that unusual? ❞

It can be difficult to know when your period is "too heavy." After all, if the first couple of days of your period require pad or tampon changes every two to three hours, and you're trying to get through a school day or enjoy a long movie, that can seem heavy enough, thank you very much!

Blobs and clots are pretty normal, but medical guidelines say that a person has "heavy menstrual bleeding" when their periods are heavy enough to interfere with their physical, social, emotional, or material quality of life.

In other words, when consistent, heavy, or prolonged periods regularly get in the way of going out, studying, hobbies, activities, and having fun, or if they are causing physical complications such as iron deficiency, then they meet the medical definition of "heavy."

HOW HEAVY IS TOO HEAVY?

If your periods are lasting longer than eight days every month, or you have to change pads or tampons every hour, or you get up through the night on most nights of your period to change tampons or pads, or you're having blood clots that are larger than a dollar coin—then your period is too heavy, and it's worth talking to your doctor about your options.

Why do some people get periods that are too heavy?

The causes of "heavy menstrual bleeding" are often different for adolescents than for older women. For adolescents, here are the causes of heavy periods —listed roughly in order from most common to least:

★ **Going through puberty:** In adolescents, heavy bleeding can be due to hormonal fluctuations and imbalances, which are part of the puberty chain that can also cause periods to disappear. (I told you it was confusing!)

★ **Polycystic ovary syndrome (PCOS):** There is a condition known as polycystic ovary syndrome (PCOS) that can cause irregular periods, and these periods can be light or really heavy. (More on PCOS on page 140.)

★ **Thyroid gland problems:** An underactive thyroid gland is a less common cause of heavy periods. The thyroid gland is a small, fleshy gland that sits at the front of your neck below your voice box. It makes hormones that help control your body's metabolism and the way your body uses its fuel (food and nutrition) to expend energy. This might not seem to have much to do with periods, but in fact all the hormone systems in the body interact in some way with each other. If something goes wrong with the thyroid gland, it can affect your periods.

* **A problem with the blood-clotting system:** A rare cause of heavy bleeding in adolescents is a problem with the body's blood-clotting system. Imagine that you cut your finger: it will bleed, but within a few minutes the bleeding stops and forms a blood clot. During a period, tiny blood vessels in the lining of the uterus leak blood while the lining sheds. Like bleeding from a skin cut, the usual blood-clotting mechanism in the body kicks in during a period so that these blood vessels don't leak indefinitely. However, there are medical conditions (such as a genetic clotting disorder) where a person's blood clots too much, or not enough.

* **Growths inside the uterus:** Problems inside the uterus can cause heavy menstrual bleeding. There are a few types of growths that affect the muscle layer of the uterus, or the lining itself, which can lead to bleeding. These usually affect older women and are extremely rare in adolescents.

* **Pregnancy:** This would go to the top of the list if you are sexually active. Even though pregnancy usually causes periods to stop (see page 133),

bleeding during pregnancy can be a sign of a miscarriage, which is not uncommon. If pregnancy is possible, it's easy to rule it out as the cause for heavy bleeding with a simple test.

★ **No obvious cause:** Sometimes, girls have heavy menstrual

bleeding and nothing shows up in any of the tests. Heavy bleeding in this situation is thought to be related to a disturbance of the way blood would normally start to clot inside the lining of the uterus when it sheds during a period.

WHAT HAPPENS IF I HAVE REALLY HEAVY PERIODS?

It's often helpful to bring the heavy bleeding under control using medication to stop the regular blood loss. Losing too much blood each month can lead to iron deficiency, which can cause tiredness and difficulty concentrating.

It's good to see a doctor, who will look into the possible causes and might do blood tests and maybe an ultrasound to look at the ovaries and uterus.

Polycystic ovary syndrome (PCOS)

❝I'm a 15-year-old girl and I get excessive hair on my face and body, a lot of pimples on my back (and quite a few on my face), and irregular periods. Could this mean I have a hormonal imbalance? If I got the problem fixed by going on the Pill, would the excessive hair and pimples go away? Please help! ❞

PCOS is something that affects quite a lot of people, but I want to give you one piece of advice right upfront: if you look stuff up on the internet about PCOS, make sure that (a) it's a trustworthy source and (b) the information you read is relevant to teenagers.

PCOS looks different in adolescents than in adults — the reason being that it can take the body at least two years to find its own pattern of menstrual cycles. So please remember: the information on the internet can make a whole lot of teenagers worry for nothing!

WHAT IS PCOS?

PCOS is a condition where there are certain interactions between the menstrual hormones and other hormones in the body, including testosterone (one of the sex hormones that's much higher in males) and insulin, which is related to controlling sugar levels in the bloodstream.

A useful way to think of PCOS is as a kind of hormone imbalance. This imbalance leads to a bunch of symptoms. PCOS affects about 1 percent of teenagers.

How do you know if you have PCOS?

Diagnosing PCOS is different for adolescents and adults. In adults, PCOS is diagnosed by having irregular periods, excessive body hair or acne, and seeing lots of mini-cysts on the ovaries on an ultrasound. Cysts are fluid-filled pouches. Throughout adolescence, the ovaries are still maturing and naturally have what looks like lots of little cysts. These can get mistaken for being polycystic (aka "lots of cysts") when they're not. Therefore, an ultrasound of the ovaries should NOT be done on adolescents to diagnose PCOS.

So there are different criteria if you're a teenager:

★ Irregular periods in adolescents: if it's been about three years since your very first period, and periods are more than 35 days or less than 21 days apart, they are defined as irregular.

★ Signs of excessive testosterone-like hormone effects on the skin: excessive body or facial hair, persistent acne that's hard to treat, or hair loss on the scalp.

What happens if you have PCOS?

Adults with PCOS tend not to ovulate regularly, which impacts their fertility, and they often gain weight. This can lead to problems with the way their body's insulin works, and therefore affect blood sugar.

The recommended treatment for adolescents with PCOS is the Pill, which restores some of the hormone balance and the symptoms associated with this. Regular exercise might also be important. Depending on sugar and insulin levels in the blood, other treatments might also be recommended.

IF YOU'RE WORRIED THAT YOU HAVE PCOS, OR WANT TO LEARN MORE, START BY VISITING YOUR DOCTOR.

Tampons and toxic shock syndrome

66 I heard about something called TSS? Is there a way to treat it? 99

Toxic shock syndrome (TSS) is caused by a particular type of bacterial infection where the bacteria (germs) produce a toxin.

TSS is extremely rare. The infection can happen in other parts of the body, and can affect anyone (children, adults, men . . . not just bleeders), but TSS was associated with the use of super-absorbent tampons (which are no longer available), especially when left inside the vagina for several hours, allowing the bacteria to multiply and release a toxin. Symptoms are usually a high fever, vomiting, diarrhea, a rash, muscle aches, and headaches. If it is not treated, TSS can lead to "shock" — a drop in blood pressure, confusion, and kidney failure.

Though rare, TSS is a medical emergency and must be treated in a hospital with antibiotics and fluids. To help avoid it, be sure to change your tampon at least every eight hours and wash your hands before and after. If you have trouble remembering to change your tampon, try setting an alarm on your phone.

My periods are so painful they affect my daily life

66 When I get my period, I have unbearable pain . . . I can't do anything and I get very sick. I've seen my doctor and she thinks the blood is going back up through the fallopian tubes. **99**

66 I'm 15 and have had my period since I was 11. I'm always in constant pain throughout the whole week of my period. I have gone to my doctor and gotten prescription pills to help with the pain, but they don't seem to work. **99**

First of all, sorry that you're going through this. It's no fun.

It might help to know you're not alone: about 10 percent of adolescents with period pain experience it with such severity that they regularly miss school, work, and other activities.

This sucks majorly!

Any period pain that causes life to come to a grinding halt, or is simply unbearable, deserves to be thoroughly checked out.

There are plenty of reasons to feel confident that what you're experiencing does not have to be your life — a doctor will be able to help.

There might not be an underlying cause, but there are treatments that do help (see page 93).

Keep track of your symptoms and where they occur on your monthly cycle (see "Keeping Track," page 58) and bring this info to your appointment. Also be prepared to push back on well-meaning parents or caregivers who tell you that "this is normal" or "you just have to suck it up." You know what you're going through better than anyone else.

It's sometimes hard to know what you're feeling when it's new — talking to your friends or trusted grown-ups can really help you figure it out!

Endometriosis

Endometriosis is a common condition in which tissue that is similar to the lining of the uterus grows outside of it, usually on other pelvic organs. It affects 5 to 10 percent of teenagers and young women. The most common symptom is pain — period pain that doesn't get better with painkillers or prescription treatment, pain that persists for days, pain that can come at other times of the menstrual cycle but feels like period pain (without the bleeding).

Endometriosis is a very individual condition, but some people have chronic pain that's awful and doesn't go away with the usual treatments (see page 96). If you suspect that you might have endometriosis, talk to your doctor right away so that they can figure out how to help you.

I grew up in a small country town and all the doctors were friends with my dad. There was NO WAY that I wanted their advice on periods, nor did I want to be in any situation where they'd be looking at my vagina. *I get it.* Trust me, I get it. So here's the thing: you're growing up, and that means you're being put in charge of your body. You're the boss! To run her body well, the boss needs good advice, and good advice comes from a good doctor. Bosses can't go it alone, so even though it might feel strange right now, get a doctor, have their number in your phone or planner, and if you need to chat, make the call. *Yumi*

PERIODS AND SEX

There's a chance that you're not up to this point in your life yet, but it's definitely interesting and worth knowing about.

Could I have sex while I have my period?

Yes, if you want to! It's the same as sex at any other time of your menstrual cycle, except you would need to remove your tampon or menstrual cup first, and there would be some blood to wipe up afterward. And you would definitely need all the usual protections against pregnancy and sexually transmitted diseases.

Can I still get pregnant while I'm menstruating?

Yes, you can get pregnant as a result of having intercourse during your period. Having your period does not rule out the risk of pregnancy, as sperm can live for up to five days inside the uterus and fallopian tubes. And sometimes you can ovulate early in your menstrual cycle. If you don't want to risk pregnancy, use protection such as condoms, or find out about other types of contraception. Condoms have the added bonus of protecting against sexually transmitted diseases.

I DON'T WANT TO HAVE SEX ON MY PERIOD

Then don't. It is literally illegal to force someone to have sex when they don't want to.

I accidentally left my tampon in during intercourse!

Whoops! This isn't ideal, since the tampon gets pushed up high, which makes it harder to remove, and it might feel uncomfortable.

If you have accidentally left a tampon in during intercourse, make sure you take it out right after. If you have any problems getting it out, it's OK to go to the doctor and ask for help removing it. But don't freak out — this has happened many times before. *You will be OK.*

147

THE INCREDIBLE MONTHLY HORMONE CYCLE

This book is mainly about getting your period, but the whole menstrual cycle is also pretty cool!

TIP We count the first day of your period as Day One of your cycle.

What goes on in a monthly hormone (menstrual) cycle?

Remember how we talked about why people get periods? It's the body's way of preparing for a future pregnancy. The menstrual cycle is a lot about that preparation. To help get our heads around it, we divide the menstrual cycle into two halves, or "phases."

In the first half, hormones from the brain are signaling the ovaries to make more hormones that will ripen an egg.

In the second half, after the ripened egg is released (known as "ovulation"), there's a small window of time during which the lining of the uterus waits for that egg to be fertilized or joined up with sperm. Fertilization is also known as conception.

If conception doesn't happen — and that's most of the time, because we are not pregnant very often — hormone levels adjust again. Then, around two weeks after ovulation, the lining sheds, and *that's* when you get your period.

PHASE 1: Egg ripening

There's actually a competition that goes on each month: a few eggs-to-be are contenders, and they begin the ripening process. But by about day eight of the cycle, one egg has dominated. It gets to ripen fully, and it is the one to travel to the uterus on around day 14–16 (depending on the length of your cycle — it's often longer in younger teens). Eggs are very tiny — about the size of the period at the end of this sentence.

To help this process, there is a rapid increase in the level of estrogen, one of the main menstrual-cycle hormones. Estrogen helps with egg ripening and preparing the lining of the uterus, but it also changes the texture of the mucus that's made by your cervix. The mucus becomes thin, runny, and clear, and you might notice this more than other discharge throughout the month — mainly because it's runnier.

Your egg has been ripening in its own special "house," also known as the ovary. When that house gets all the right signals, it "opens the door" and lets the egg out. This is called *ovulation*. Some people feel a sharp pain when this happens, and some might even notice a spot of blood. It's usually very short-lived. Some people experience an increase in sex drive around the time of ovulation, and it's thought that this is to encourage the creation of babies.

The egg's journey

Once an egg has been released, it only has a couple of days to live . . . unless it meets a sperm. Fertilization (when the egg and sperm join) is the very first step in making a baby. Most eggs — whether they're the ones in the ovaries or the ones that are released once puberty is underway — do *not* make babies.

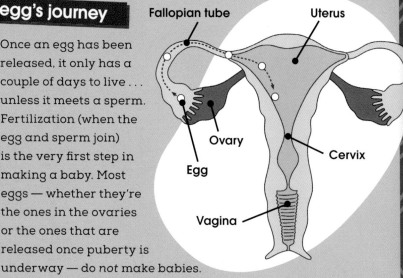

That is nature's course. Same with sperm — millions get made, but very few go on to make babies.

   If an egg is not fertilized, it simply dissolves inside the fallopian tube.

Once the egg has been released

After ovulation — the release of the ripened egg by the ovary — the level of estrogen dramatically drops for about a week, but then picks up again a bit. At the same time, another type of menstrual hormone, progesterone, increases. Progesterone makes the mucus from the cervix thick and sticky. You might notice discharge like that on your underwear during this time in your cycle — different from when your egg was ripening.

The "premenstrual" blues

Research has looked at how the menstrual hormones affect our emotions, thoughts, and moods. The dip in estrogen and rise in progesterone in the second half of the menstrual cycle seem to have an effect on mood for some people. Many people feel irritable, depressed, or anxious before they menstruate, or have trouble regulating emotions — this can lead to fights or feelings of grumpiness toward others.

Other premenstrual symptoms related to hormones include breast tenderness, bloating, headaches, food cravings, increased appetite, and joint and muscle pains.

The big clue to figuring out if these are related to the menstrual cycle is if the symptoms only appear after ovulation, and disappear when your period starts. See page 92 for information on premenstrual syndrome (PMS).

PERIOD BOSS
Pledge

All Period Bosses know:
KNOWLEDGE IS POWER! The more info you have about your period, the better.

A Period Boss **DOES NOT JUDGE** how other people manage their periods. If you prefer pads, tampons, period panties, or whatever, that's fine. Your body. Your choice. Zero judgies.

A Period Boss understands that being "grossed out" by periods helps no one.

A PERIOD BOSS TRIES TO ALWAYS HAVE EXTRA PADS/TAMPONS IN THEIR PERIOD PACK AND IS WILLING TO GIVE THEM TO A FELLOW BOSS IN NEED.

A Period Boss can dutifully perform a pants check for leaks if asked. Even if asked by a total stranger.

EXPAND YOUR PERIOD VOCABULARY!

ACETAMINOPHEN

A pain relief medication that is thought to work in the brain to reduce the feeling of pain.

APPLICATOR

A plastic or cardboard tube that comes with some tampons to help with insertion.

BLOOD CLOT

A clump of blood that has become solid — a bit like jelly — that sometimes comes out during your period.

CERVIX

The lower, narrower part of the uterus.

THE PILL

CONTRACEPTIVE

Something that is intended to stop pregnancy. Can take many forms — condom, implant, IUD, and the Pill, to name a few.

CRAMP

A painful muscle spasm that can occur during your period.

154

CYCLE

Refers to the menstrual cycle — the pattern of changes that your hormones, ovaries, and uterus go through repeatedly once you get your period.

DISCHARGE

Fluid that comes out of your vagina; the fluid may be clear and runny or white and sticky.

EGG

The reproductive cell released from an ovary about once a month after you start getting your period.

DYSPHORIA

A state of feeling unhappy, dissatisfied, or uneasy. Gender dysphoria is when a person experiences distress because their gender identity does not match other people's expectations of them.

ENDOMETRIOSIS

A common condition in which tissue that is similar to the lining of the uterus grows outside it.

ENDORPHINS

Feel-good hormones that can reduce your perception of pain.

HEAVY FLOW

Refers to the level of your period blood flow — if there's more, it's heavy!

IBUPROFEN

An anti-inflammatory pain relief medication. It works by countering a period hormone called prostaglandin that can lead to muscle cramps.

LIGHT FLOW

Refers to the level of your period blood flow. If there's less, it's light!

MENOPAUSE

The time when your reproductive system shuts down and you can no longer make a baby in your body.

MENSES

The blood and other matter that is discharged from the vagina during menstruation, aka "period"!

MENSTRUAL PRODUCTS (OR SANITARY ITEMS)

Collective name for pads, tampons, cups, and other things that collect your period.

MENSTRUATION

The regular discharge of menses through the vagina.

PREMENSTRUAL SYNDROME (PMS)

The physical symptoms and feelings you can experience before your period.

MISGENDERING

When others refer to a person as being a gender that is not how they identify (for example, calling someone "she" if they identify as "he" and vice versa).

POLYCYSTIC OVARY SYNDROME (PCOS)

A condition that can cause irregular periods that may be light or really heavy.

PROSTAGLANDIN

The period hormone that can cause cramps, nausea, and more pooping during periods!

PUBERTY

A time of hormonal changes that cause growth and change in body shape, as well as the start of fertility and sexual maturation.

SHEDDING

The natural and regular removal of the lining of the uterus — your period!

SPOTTING

Small spots of blood, sometimes outside of your regular period time.

THYROID

A gland that secretes the hormones that relate to the way your body uses fuel and energy.

WINGS

The sticky tabs on the side of pads that stick to your underwear to keep the pad in place and reduce the risk of leaks.

VULVA

The genital area that includes the pad of tissue above your pubic bone, the inner and outer lips around the vagina, the clitoris, urethra opening, and the area at the opening of the vagina.

RESOURCES

Want to learn even more? Here are some suggestions!

Call

Office on Women's Health 1-800-994-9662

Planned Parenthood 1-800-230-7526

Follow

@happyperiodorg (Twitter)

@thepadproject (Instagram)

@freeperiods (Instagram)

@wearehappyperiod (Instagram)

@menstrualhealthhub (Instagram)

@periodmovement

#menstrualmovement

#freebleeding

#periodpower

#endperiodpoverty

#menstruationmatters

#periodpositive

#periodpowerful

Listen and learn

Stuff Mom Never Told You podcast

The Flow Down podcast

The Heavy Flow podcast

PERIOD podcast

Track

Clue

Period Tracker

Flo

MagicGirl

Cycles

Eve

Watch

Period. End of Sentence.

Period Stories

100 Years of Periods

Resist

bloodygoodperiod.com

daysforgirls.org

period.org

PERIOD Proud
ANYTHING YOU CAN DO, I CAN DO BLEEDING
THE BRAVE AND THE BLEEDING
PERIODS ARE NOT A LUXURY
GO WITH THE FLOW
GROW THROUGH WHAT YOU GO THROUGH

ACKNOWLEDGMENTS

Thank you to Claudine Ryan, the producer at ABC who formed, captained, and championed the *Ladies, We Need to Talk* podcast team, which led me to many brilliant things, including to Dr. Melissa Kang. Thank you, Marisa Pintado, for knowing there was a book in Melissa and me and helping us to excavate it. Thank you to all the people who shared their stories about bleeding, especially those who share within these pages: Amelia Lush, Amy, Anouk Ely, Audrey, Chloe Prideaux, Cymone Rose, Dee Dee Ely, Hsin-Ju Ely (Raw), Itsuko Dohi, Kathryn Scott, Lisa, Marihuzka Cornelius, Max, "Nadine," Nevo Zisin, Samantha Simmons, Soreti Kadir, Stella Barton, and Tannah Skye. There are others whose stories maybe didn't make the text but were freakin' cool and useful anyway — I'm looking at you, Evie, Jenish, Maria Lugaro, and Carla Mico, and every other bleeding sister. Thanks to the team at Hardie Grant Egmont, including Penelope White, Pooja Desai, and Emma Schwarcz, and the greatest team ever of Benython Oldfield and Jenny Latham. Big thanks to Martin Bendeler for laughing at my jokes, and to my mom, Yoshiko, for being so shy about periods that I had no choice but to find inspiration. Thank you to all the sisters, the fighters, and the warrior women. And thanks to everyone who ever helped out a stranger in a restroom stall when they were caught in a bind!

Yumi

Thank you to Claudine Ryan and to Yumi for coming and talking to me one day in my office about some things that ladies need to talk about. It was the start of an incredible ride, along with Marisa Pintado and the Hardie Grant Egmont team — Penelope White, Emma Schwarcz, and Pooja Desai, the wonderfully talented Jenny Latham, and Benython Oldfield. The ride also took me back to my past self and those of my own period allies, whose friendship and common sense made it all OK. Thanks to Mitchell Smith, for having my back and enjoying the ride with me. My expert reviewers have been invaluable — Moya Keating, Maddie H., Dr. Deborah Bateson, Professor Rachel Skinner, Professor Kate Steinbeck, and Sukriti Dabral: thank you with all my heart. Thank you to all the *Dolly* magazine editors and staff from 1993 to 2016 for giving me the privilege of hearing from a whole generation of tweens and teens: nothing is or ever can be as authentic or poignant as their own voices.

Dr. Melissa

ABOUT THE ILLUSTRATOR

Jenny Latham is an illustrator from the United Kingdom. She has a passion for illustrating real women and hopes to empower others through her work. Jenny hopes that one day talking about periods won't be so taboo and that girls will be able to speak up about their bodies and not be ashamed to be whoever they want to be.

That's it!
YOU'RE READY!
Come back when
you need us!

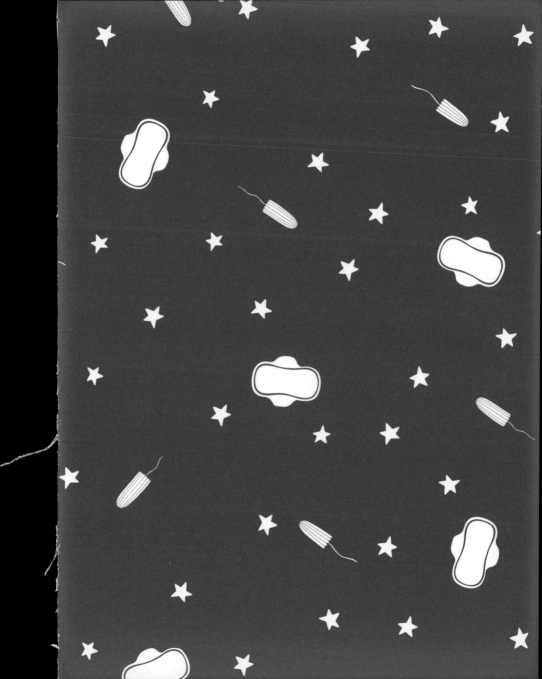

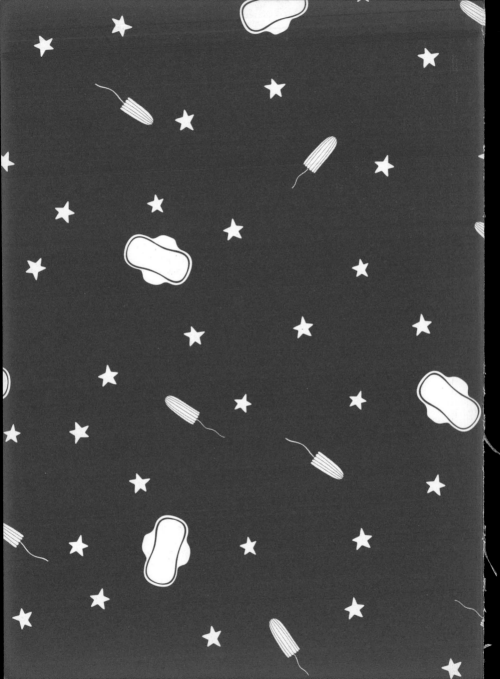